MW00679934

The Fastest Growing Religion on Earth:
How Genealogy Captured the Brains
and Imaginations of Americans

by

Doug Bremner

Published by

Laughing Cow Books

The Fastest Growing Religion on Earth: How Genealogy Captured the Brains and Imaginations of Americans

Copyright © 2013 by Doug Bremner

ISBN 978-0-9833270-6-6

Published in Atlanta, GA, by Laughing Cow Books.

Cover art by Sabina Vaccarino Bremner.

Printed by JM Multimedia Designs and East Atlanta Copy Center, Atlanta, GA.

This book is dedicated to my wife, Viola, and my children Sabina and Dylan, who tolerated my genealogy addiction while it lasted. This book is also dedicated to Charles Hansen and the volunteer "genies" of the Eastern Washington Genealogical Society, who tirelessly volunteer to help genealogy addicts get their fix, and who made my quest a possibility.

All rights reserved. Without limiting the rights under copyright reserved above, no part of this publication may be reproduced, stored in or introduced into a retrieval system, or transmitted, in any form, or by any means (electronic, mechanical, photocopying, recording, or otherwise) without the prior written permission of both the copyright owner and the above publisher of this book.

Books by Doug Bremner

Does Stress Damage the Brain?
Understanding Trauma-related
Disorders From a Mind-Body
Perspective

Brain Imaging Handbook

Before You Take That Pill: Why the
Drug Industry May Be Bad For Your
Health

The Goose That Laid the Golden Egg:
Accutane – the truth that had to be told

You can find links to purchase all books
at:

www.dougbremner.com/laughingco
wbooks.html

Table of Contents

Introduction

For millions of Americans, the quest to find one's
ancestors has become an obsession. For others, it
is literally a religion. After writing a book about
the history of his family, the author realized that
half of it was missing, literally. This is the story
about how he found the other half, and what he
learned along the way about the history and
practice of genealogy, his fellow genealogy
fanatics, and himself.

Chapter 1

Carved into the solid granite of a mountain in the Wasatch Mountain Range, located in the Little Cottonwood Canyon, twenty miles southeast of Salt Lake City, Utah, is a place that stores information about the births, marriages and deaths, of over two billion people. It's the largest single database on the details of the human race in the world.

Is this the United States Government? Is this the Federal Bureau of Investigation? Is this the United Nations?

No, this is the Church of Jesus Christ of Latter Day Saints. The LDS Church, also known as the Mormons, has created a place to file away records about births, marriages, and deaths of two billion people. Buried 600 feet into the mountain, protected by two nine ton and one 14 ton doors that were built to withstand a nuclear blast, the LDS church is squirreling away information at an incredible clip in a place called the Granite Mountain Vault.

Granite Mountain is the place where the Mormons quarried the marble that they used to build their massive temples in Salt Lake.

Their goal is to hoard all of the available information on the ancestors of all of the members of the church, and everyone else on the planet, if they can get away with it, based on their fundamental belief that sooner or later everyone will logically convert to the true church. Five billion documents have been stored on 1 ½ million rolls of microfilm and 1 ½ million microfiche. 25,000 volunteers are currently working to scan and index all of these documents, so that one day (and one day soon), you can access all of this data while sitting in your kitchen in your slippers with a laptop on your lap.

And how do they organize this army of volunteers to enter all of this data?

Genealogy is not just for your Great Aunt anymore. Genealogy is catching on as one of America's latest fads, with lots of 30- and 40-somethings tapping data into their genealogical programs.

The LDS church has a system, where you can access a web site, and a scanned record of a list of recorded births from a 19th Century church in rural Alabama, or a list of recorded burials at a 18th century cemetery in Edinburgh, Scotland, will pop up on your screen. Your job is to type in the names and dates as you see them.

Somewhere else on the planet, someone else is typing in the same information. If there is a discrepancy between what you and that other person typed in, the record is automatically forwarded to a genealogical expert, who makes a final decision about how the name should be recorded.

And it's not just the Mormons that are into genealogy. Millions of Americans outside the LDS church are trolling the scanned census records, ship passenger lists, and obituaries, looking for their ancestors. These people have grown to think that learning more about their families is not such a bad idea. In fact, for some, it has become an obsession.

As I was writing these words, I got an automated phone call from Bank of America. There was an unusual pattern of activity on my credit card, they said.

A helpful woman came on the line. "Did you make a charge to myfamily.com?"

That was the online company that allowed people to login to their family web site and update their family tree, share photos, and say happy birthday to their cousins.

"That's OK," I said.

"U.S. Search?"

"That's fine."

That was the online service that could track down people, even if the address you had on them was twenty years old. It would tell you if they paid their phone bill on time or spent time in jail, and give you an aerial photo of their house. Then you could cold call them and ask about your family ancestors.

"Vitalrecordcheck.com?"

That was where I had ordered the death certificate of one of my possible relatives online.

"That's fine."

"AWT.com? This looks like a genealogy site. $9.99 every month?"

"Yes, that's ancestry world tree. I have a regular subscription to that."

"OK, well you have an account with a $17,000 limit, and we just want to make sure that the activity on the account is legitimate."

"Everyone looks fine, thanks for calling," I said.

As I hung up the phone I thought about what the woman had said. *There is a pattern of unusual activity on your credit card.* I had had a sudden and unusual change in my purchasing behavior.

What did she think had happened? Had my credit card been stolen? Or had something happened to me that had caused me to change my buying behavior? What could that be?

An addiction?

I didn't know what else to call it.

As I lived through the various forms of what I later realized was an addiction, I became fascinated with the process. What drove millions of apparently sane people to spend hours of their free time scouring through musty record books and peering into the dark glass of a microfilm machine, when they could be outside having a good time? What was it that caused otherwise normal people to build websites with hundreds, thousands, and tens of thousands of names? Who didn't stop when they traced their ancestors, but kept on going until they had traced all of the descendants of their ancestors, or all of the descendants of that ancestor?

Was gazing into the past driven by the same forces that gives us pleasure at staring into the distance from a mountain top, or while out at sea? Was it just narcissism, or vanity, or a desire to avoid thinking about the pain and unpleasantness of daily life?

Do we have an innate tendency to connect with the spirits of our ancestors, something called "ancestor worship," or "veneration of the ancestors," that goes by another name in Asian cultures, which is probably not translatable? Could this innate tendency be triggered into overdrive by a random encounter with rootsweb.com? Or are there forgotten souls of our ancestors, lonely in their abandoned cemeteries by the side of a country road, who want us to find them? Do they need our help, or do we need theirs? Or was all this genealogy stuff just a desire to connect with others, or to understand or feel more grounded in ones self? Could it be in part all of these things, and more?

This book is an attempt to answer those questions, told through the prism of the story of my own genealogy addiction, and the stories of others whose genealogical universes I came to co-inhabit.

Two thousand mile east of the LDS's Salt Lake City Temple, which towers over Temple Square, the spires of the "Duke Chapel" similarly lord it over the quad of Duke University. Although built for the glory of Methodism, as opposed to Mormonism, the architecture of both buildings is designed to promote the feeling that you are reaching from the mortal sphere toward the heavens. It was to this temple of knowledge that I repaired in 1983, the product of a small town in the West, a naïve boy who had attended his senior prom with a girl who was a baptized member of the LDS church.

Things at Duke didn't go exactly as I had planned. After failing my Biochemistry class, I wanted to go back to the homeland, Washington State, for a breather.

My family had lived there for four generations. After his discharge from the Union Army of the Civil War, my Scottish born ancestor, James Bremner, married a woman from Massachusetts, named Abigail Clark Freeman. They moved out West to the Washington Territory, got their forty acre "homestead" land, and went to work cutting down and burning the massive fir trees to clear out the land. They started a farm and built a log cabin. They called the place "Delta". It's a few miles from the current town of Lynden, Washington, right up against the Canadian border.

Abigail came from a long line of Cape Codders that stretched back to Plymouth and the Mayflower. She was a woman whom James had never met, but whom he had spent years writing letters to while he was a soldier in the Union Army, and she was a daughter of a Cape Cod whaling boat captain from Brewster, Massachusetts.

My grandfather remembered Abigail, his grandmother, as a woman who did a lot of knitting, and not much talking.

Abigail Clark Freeman Bremner, Powell River BC, c 1900

The family legend was that James was wounded in the battle of Antietam. However, using the genealogy skills I learned in the course of my new quest, I wrote to the National Archives and got his discharge papers, which stated that he had served in the Union Army, pushing carts of wounded soldiers. He was discharged from active duty, only a few months after he enlisted, when he hurt his back pushing his cart in Vicksburg. He spent the rest of the war recuperating in Washington, D.C. It didn't look like he had ever fired a single shot in the Civil War, let alone come out as a war hero.

Here is what I knew about my family tree.

http://www.bremnerhistory.com/fig1.jpg

Family Tree for Doug Bremner

5 Generations

You can see that half of it is missing.

That is because my mother, Laurnell Cooper Bremner, who died suddenly of meningitis when I was four years old, was adopted by Lyndle and Madeline Cooper, two school teachers from Eastern Washington, at birth.

I arranged to go back to Seattle for a research year with my uncle, who was working in

14

reproductive endocrinology at the University of Washington.

I moved to Seattle and rented an apartment on Capital Hill, near the downtown. My superficial reason for coming back was that I was burnt out, but the real reason was that I hadn't wrapped up all of my loose ends. There were many facets of my past that were holding me back, many unanswered questions. I wanted answers to those questions.

As one of my psychiatry professors at Duke later told me, "If you leave some of your troops fighting a battle behind the lines, you won't have enough strength to win the battle at the front lines." In my case my troops were all over the map, some of them running for the nearest cover of trees.

The death of my mother was catching up with me.

I decided to write a history of my family. My grandparents, George Archibald Bremner II and Marian Bay Bremner, were in their late 80s, and it was not known how long they would live. Now was the time to get down in writing the wealth of knowledge that they had from the past 150 years, transmitted through their own parents and grandparents. They were living alone on the family farm in Lynden, Washington, placed in the vast flat floodplain of the Nooksack River, whose periodic floods were the source of the great fertility of that region, like all of the river valleys in that area.

During the day I worked on a research project with my Uncle. At night and on weekends I spent time writing the book about my family, and more importantly picking up on the missing details about my own life.

This quest did not come out of the blue. My ancestors in the male line had a tradition of writing a brief autobiography of their lives, going back to my great grandfather, who first rode the train across America in 1880, and later was paddled by Indians up the Nooksack River to their 40 acre homestead in Whatcom County near the Canadian border. To accomplish this task I first set out to re-visit the homeland, Lynden, Washington, and Whatcom County, an area abutting the Canadian border, a flat land periodically flooded by the Nooksack River, once filled with massive fir trees and the only humans the Indians who lived along the river's edge pulling their subsistence in salmon from their fish traps, and burying their dead by placing them in canoes that they put on top of the highest tree branches.

Now the mighty trees have been flattened and burned away by my ancestors and others, in their hope of obtaining a stable patch of ground that would sustain their families, and give them a sense of peace and security and see them through their older years.

The land is so flat and fertile that it drew the Dutchmen like itinerant laborers, who smell a good home cooked meal, and come wandering back to the table to a land that reminded them of their own, and now the land is filled with tidy Dutch dairy farms with their little signs in the front yard that show the prizes they have won for having the most tidy farm in the county. This land runs so flat that all the roads run straight like arrows until they turn at right angles at the border of the next farmer's property, running east until they hit the North Cascade Mountains, where the farm land is spent, and the mountains rise up and up until they meet the foothills of the North Cascade Mountains. This is the hardy land where my grandfather worked as an itinerant logger, and the hills where he drove us as children to pick salmon berries and breathe the clean mountain air.

I spent many weekends in Lynden where I interviewed my grandparents and tried to obtain as much information as possible about my family life. My grandmother faithfully served me milk (from their cow) and cookies (the special home-baked potato chip kind that were always faithfully there in their plastic containers on the kitchen table of my grandparents house from as far as I can remember). My grandfather had carefully kept clippings about every aspect of our family history so it was up to me to put it all together.

They also had some stories for me about my mother.

Here is a picture from about twenty years ago of my grandfather, standing outside the barn on the family farm, with my wife and kids.

It seems that my great-grandmother,
Madeline Ella Rockey Bay, had developed an
interest in genealogy back about 1900. Her
method was to write letters to distant cousins in
the Rockey family from Pennsylvania, Illinois,
and other points in the Rockey family diaspora.

These letters became like circular letters, in that someone would respond, and then transcribe on the typewriter all of the other related letters on the subject.

Madeline "Ella" Rockey Bay

My grandfather gave me copies of the *Clark-Clarke Genealogy,* which outlined the genealogy of the Clarks, a Cape Cod family who claimed descent from Thomas Clarke, a shipmate on the *Mayflower* (however a genealogy authority later disputed that claim, saying that there was not evidence that a later emigrant to Plymouth Colony named Thomas Clarke was the same man who was on the *Mayflower.* Another Cape Cod family in my line was the Freemans, who had their own genealogy. I was able later to trace the ancestors of Abigail Clark Freeman, my great-great-great- grandmother, and the Cape Cod product of the Freemans and Clarks, and determine that she was descended from a passenger of the *Mayflower,* although it wasn't Thomas Clarke.

My grandfather also gave me *History of the Plymale Family* by Fred Plymale. This book was full of family trees, transcribed letters, and other facts about the Plymale family, which include Louisa Plymale, who in 1863 married Thomas John Bay in Crown City, a small town on the Ohio River in the State of Ohio, and who was my grandmother's grandmother. As my grandmother, Marian Bay Bremner, began to write letters to her distant Plymale cousins, she started to learn things that she didn't want to know about. For example, that the Plymales were from the South, and many of them were fervent secessionists in the Civil War. As someone who always identified her family as being part of the North, this was something she didn't want to know about.

As noted in a letter transcribed by Fred Plymale in the *History of the Plymale Family* written by a descendant of one of the Plymales who fought for the South.

"My grandfather was taken as a prisoner of war by the Yankees. He survived by eating rats in prison. He never talked much about the war. But he was one red hot REBEL."

I think this was too much for my grandmother.

In my fact finding expedition I also went to talk to other family members. I visited my uncle Bill, who was a medical doctor and medical researcher at the University of Washington in Seattle. He lived on a funky hippie-style homestead with a lot of apple trees and wild blackberry vines on Vashon Island in the middle of Puget Sound and took the ferry every day to go to work. I went to have dinner with himself and his wife, Jane, who traveled across the country from her home in Bellingham, Washington, to be a student at Boston University so she could be close to her sweetheart who had been admitted to Harvard University from the humble origins of Lynden Washington High School. She didn't like it there very much, in fact neither of them liked it there very much, my uncle constantly suffered from the fact that he couldn't afford the clothes that the blue bloods were wearing. But unlike Bill Gates he did not drop out of Harvard, and he later went on to become internationally known for his medical research and to become head of the Medicine Department in Seattle. They were able to tell me important information about the early years with my mother and things about my mother I didn't know before. My grandparents also provided important information about my mother from their own memories and history.

I sat at my typewriter for many nights in my small apartment on Capital Hill in Seattle that year, typing out family trees and the history of my family. It was a labor of love. Love for my grandparents, who I knew would die in a few years, taking the history of my family with them. Love for a way of life, filled with apple pressings, hymns sung in church, and going further back house raisings, and other rituals.

I called my book *The History of the Bremner Family* and took it to a printer to make 100 copies in hard cover to sell to my family. At that time fronting the money for the publication costs was quite a reach. I sent out a flyer to the other members of the family to promote it. In typical Scotch fashion, some of them complained about the price.

After I went back to my regular life, medical school, residency, the pursuit of my career, I found that I wasn't satisfied with my life. I felt that I needed to know more about who I was, where I had come from, the events that had shaped my life. The *History of the Bremner Family* was not enough. I decided that I needed to know more.

Chapter 2

In the early 1990s, Cyndi Howells, a housewife from Puyallup, Washington, and a member of the Tacoma-Pierce County (Washington) Genealogical Society, walked in to the annual meeting of the Washington State Genealogical Society, which was being held in her home town. Dressed in a bathrobe and her bathroom slippers, she held up a disk in her right hand.

"I've got twenty files on here," she shouted to the assembled amateur genealogists. "Each file is the address of a place on the internet where you can find genealogical information. I'm going to see how many more I can find."

At the next year's annual meeting of the Washington State Genealogical Society she came back with 50 more.

And the next year she had even more.

In 1996 she had over 1,000. She called her list cyndislist, and used oznet to post it at www.cyndislist.com.

Soon she was crashing oznet, and she had to move to a different server.

Cyndislist grew with the internet to become the craigslist of the genealogy world. At last count, she had 264,800 links to different sites in 180 categories on her site, with over a 1000 new links added per month, and over 22 million visitors. With thousands of visitors a day, answering their email and working on her web site has become a full time job.

Cyndi's fame grew with her list. She went from an obscure, eccentric, amateur genealogist from Puyallup, Washington, in her bath robe and slippers, to one of the most cited, quoted, and interviewed people in the field of genealogy in the world. As *Newsweek* wrote in February 24, 1997, "The biggest boon to the heritage hunt has been cyberspace. No one has been more influential there than Cyndi Howells, a Puyallup, Wash., housewife who became obsessed with genealogy after tracing her own family tree."

That was the key word. *Obsessed*. Why else would an apparently normal person spend hours trolling the internet to look for online ship passenger lists and other trivia?

While Cyndi was first discovering the wonders of the internet, however, I was still using paper and pencil to research my genealogy. I wrote several letters to organizations that archived information about adopted children, and provided them with information about my mother, in the hope that a birth parent would check the registry.

One of them wrote back and provided the name and address of a woman named Diane Sams, in Spokane, Washington, whom they said could help me get my mother's adoption files opened.

Ms. Sams had the adoption records opened by court order, and turned those documents over to me.

I received a birth certificate in the mail. The document read "Washington State Board of Health, Bureau of Vital Statistics, Certificate of Birth, Spokane, Washington." It listed place of birth as N. 2618 Altamont. Sex of child: Female. Legitimate? No. Date of Birth: February 23, 1932. Father: Full Name: Edward Conlon. Residence: E. 2123 Central Ave. Color: White. Age at last Birthday: 26. Birthplace: unknown. Occupation: Employee Dessert Hotel. Mother: Alice Pauline Woods. Residence: N. 2618 Altamont. Color: White. Age at last birthday: 19 (years). Birthplace: Washington. Occupation: None. Number of child of this mother: First. Number of children, this mother, now living: One. Certificate of Attending Physician or Midwife: JF Hall MD, 601 Fernwell Bldg.

I also obtained the death certificate for my mother from the Department of Social and Health Services in Olympia Washington. Place of Death: King County, Seattle, DOA (Death on Arrival), University Hospital. Deceased: Laurnell Bremner. Date of Death: February 12, 1966. Age: 33. Occupation: Housewife. Birthplace: Spokane, Washington. Cause of death: Meningitis. Burial: cremation, 2/14/66. Name of cemetery: Mt. View crematory, Tacoma, Washington.

The legal papers from the adoption were as follows

IN THE SUPERIOR COURT OF THE STATE OF WASHINGTON

IN AND FOR THE COUNTY OF SPOKANE

No.2 5 9 3 1

ORDER OF ADOPTION

The above cause coming on to be heard this day in Open Court on the petition of L. R. Cooper and Madeline Cooper, his wife, for leave to adopt Jane Doe Woods, a minor, and change the name of said minor to Madeline Laurnell Cooper, and the Court having heard the testimony of L. R. Cooper and Madeline Cooper, and Edith Gilbert, and the said Madeline Cooper having been examined separately and apart from her said husband L. R. Cooper, and it appearing that the said Alice Woods, mother of the said minor child, has surrendered said child to Edith Gilbert and has filed her written consent, and that said written consent of Edith Gilbert has been filed to such adoption, and the Court having found the facts to be as follows:

I. That the petitioners, L. R. Cooper and Madeline Cooper, his wife, are residents of the County of Spokane, State of Washington.

II. That Jane Doe Woods is a minor female child of Alice Woods; and is of the age, to-wit, of two months and was born in the City of Spokane, County of Spokane, state of Washington, on the 23rd day of February, 1932; that the present whereabouts of the father of said child is unknown, said father having deserted said mother and said subsequent minor child prior to the birth of said child, and having abandoned said mother and said child during all times herein mentioned. That on and prior to the birth of said child and In the Matter of the Adoption of JANE DOE WOODS, a minor,

"Thereto the father of said minor deserted the said Alice Woods and has since not been heard from, and has at all times since continued to abandon said Alice Woods and said minor Child; that the whereabouts of said father is not now known, during all of said time said father has wholly failed to support his said family. That the, said Alice Woods and Edith Gilbert, the next friend, at all times herein mentioned have been and now are resident of Spokane County, State of Washington. That at all times since her birth, said minor child has been in the care and custody of said Edith Gilbert. And the Court being fully satisfied of the ability of said L. R. Cooper and Madeline Cooper, his wife, to properly bring up, educate and care for said minor child, and being fully satisfied or the fitness and propriety of such adoption, and being fully advised in the premises, NOW, THEREFORE, it is ORDERED, ADJUDGED, and DECREED, that, said petition for the adoption be and the same is hereby granted and that the said minor child is from this date to all legal intents and purposes the child of L. R. Cooper and Madeline Cooper, his wife, and that the name of said minor child is hereby changed Madeline Laurnell Cooper.

Done in open Court, this 20 day of May, 1932.

CHAS. H. LEAVY

Judge

FILED MAY 20, 1932

HARRY M. LUCAS, Clerk

At the bottom of these papers was a signature, testifying under legal oath that the above statements were true, and that her name was, 'Alice Pauline Woods.'

I got a hold of my mother's adoptions file in a time before ancestry.com, Cyndi Howells, and the wide-spread distribution of genealogy information on the internet. If you wanted to view a census, you basically had to go to an LDS church and request a microfilm, a service they provided for a small fee. Alternatively, you could write a letter to the government, but you still had to find a microfilm reader. The LDS church represented the easiest approach, and they never did any proselytizing.

I made several trips to my local LDS Church in the early 1990s to do family research. At that time I was an Assistant Professor of Psychiatry at Yale University School of Medicine in New Haven, CT. I was married and had two children, born in 1992 and 1997. Whenever I could steal away from work, I drove out to the LDS church in Woodbridge, a suburb of New Haven. There I ordered microfilm from the central repository in Salt Lake City, and read it on the machines in their family history library. It wasn't a rapid process. You would go out there, order the film, and come back a week later to view it on the microfiche reader.

I searched the census records for evidence of Alice Pauline Woods or Edward Conlon. I couldn't find any. I also looked for my great-great-great-grandmother, Sarah Eleanor Lee. According to the family bibles, she was the grand-daughter of Richard Henry Lee, famous for being the Virginian to move that his state should separate from England. Unfortunately, the earliest evidence of Sarah Eleanor Lee that I could find was when she arrived in Lewis (later Mason) County, Kentucky, with her husband, Augustus Wilson, in the early 1800s. After having a bunch of kids there, they moved to Shelby County, Indiana, where her husband promptly died, and where she later died. A book on the genealogy of the Lee family I found in the library of Yale University, where I was working at the time, showed no evidence of her.

However, I still had the verbal history from my Great-Aunt Olive Wilson, her great-niece, whom I remember as a child singing "Amazing Grace" in her Bellingham nursing home at the age of 102. She knew Sarah Eleanor Lee personally, and insisted that she was, indeed, the granddaughter of Richard Henry Lee.

Sarah Eleanor's son was Caleb Taylor Wilson, who married Isodore Van Treese. Here is Caleb with his family. My great-grandmother Rose Wilson, mother of my grandfather George A. Bremner II, is the one standing on the far left.

They moved west to establish a farm in Missouri where they lived for many years before continuing out West to Bellingham in the Washington Territory. Here they are on their Missouri farm.

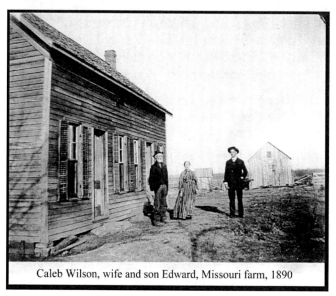

Caleb Wilson, wife and son Edward, Missouri farm, 1890

Over the course of the 90s, I learned more about the internet and how it could be used for genealogy research. In fact, it seemed the perfect medium for individuals to communicate information that had been accumulated from Aunts and Uncles about the details of family history. In 2004 I bought a book, *Teach Yourself HTML in a Weekend* and registered the web site, www.bremnerhistory.com. I registered the site after my grandfather died, and I missed the annual family reunion, or at least the idea of it. I thought this could be a "virtual family reunion," all the more appealing since, after my grandfather's death, they sold off the old family farm in Lynden, Washington, forever severing that link to the past.

I started posting the chapters of my book on the history of the Bremner family. The web site had a link to my specific email linked to the site, doug@bremnerhistory.com. I began trolling the internet, looking for like-minded enthusiasts.

And what a world I found.

Like a series of fortified castles scattered across the landscape, I found the internet to be strewn with a series of home-grown web sites like my own, each promoting a particular primary ancestor. The goal was to find others who shared a common ancestor.

My first contact was Raymond L. Maris.

Raymond and I shared a common ancestor in George Maris.

George Maris was born in England. His daughter, Alice Maris, married Jacob Simcock in Pennsylvania in 1684. Family legend stated that the Simcocks came to America with William Penn and the other Quakers who founded Pennsylvania. I reach back to Alice Maris through a long line of Simcocks who lived in Centre and Clinton Counties, Pennsylvania for over 200 years, working as laborers and farmers in the Bush and Sugar Valleys. Charlotte White Simcox, great-great-granddaughter of Alice and Jacob Simcox, married Thomas Jefferson Rockey in 1864 after he hung up his spurs from Civil War service in the First Pennsylvania Volunteer Cavalry Reserves, Company D. They moved to

Charleston, West Virginia, and later Bellingham, Washington at the end of the 19th Century.

Raymond L. Maris had a website at www.maris.net promoting his genealogy research with the following introduction: "The Maris Family in the United States, a book tracing the descendants of George (1632-1705) and Alice (surname unknown) (1632-1699) MARIS, who immigrated to Pennsylvania from England in 1683, was published in 1885. Our family has had a copy of this book since its original publication and, like many other MARIS descendants; we have long hoped that the book could someday be updated. Several years ago, at the urging of my

Thomas Jefferson Rockey

father, I decided to make an effort to at least partially update this book and have thus far added data on over 225,000 descendants in addition to the 6,000 or so included in the original book. Although I had originally planned to publish an updated book (and may yet at some time in the future), I feel that publication on the Web will allow a larger number of interested individuals more immediate, up-to-date, and economical access to the data I have gathered. I am also considering publishing the info in CD ROM format, since this would be more economical than publishing a book.

"I am anxious to hear from anyone, whether a Maris descendant or not, who is interested in obtaining additional information about their ancestors, or in helping me with additions/corrections to the data. Also, please let me know if you would be interested in a book or CD.

"The data on my GenCircles and RootsWeb websites is a subset of my off-line genealogy database, limited to 10 generations of non-living descendants of George Maris, their spouses, and spouses' parents and can be accessed by clicking on the links below. Over 170,000 individuals are included.

"In my off-line database I have information on over 400,000 individuals including over 231,000 Maris descendants. The off-line database includes information on 16 generations of descendants as well as additional ancestral information on George Maris and some spouses of descendants who were members of other Colonial Pennsylvania families or who were my personal ancestors. Most were Quakers and prominently represented families besides Maris include..."

Raymond Maris also had a list of famous descendants of George and Alice Maris, including Al Gore, Larry Bird, Glenn Close, and Buffalo

Bill, not to mention one of the founders of the Mormon Church.

This guy was really into it.

I sent Raymond an email

"Dear Raymond, I am a descendant of Charlotte Simcox who goes back to your Simcock line. I was able to pick up several new generations from your database. She left PA and went out to Washington State. You can follow out her ancestors if you want in the database called 'Bremner' on rootsweb world connect, and read about her at www.bremnerhistory.com (under Bay, the family her daughter married into)."

"Cousin Doug," he responded. "Thanks very much for writing!

"I can probably add a few more generations for you, since I have more on Charlotte's ancestry in my off-line database. Just let me know if you are interested.

"Thanks, I did take a look at your site, very nice! I also found more on Charlotte's descendants in your RootsWeb data and was hoping you could share the rest with me, including information on the living. I don't post information on the living on the web either, but I do maintain it in my off-line database for future reference.

"Thanks again, I'm looking forward to hearing more from you!"

I responded, "I don't have any objections to showing living relatives, it appears to be the way the rootsweb posted things. I attached my gedcom file, I don't know if you can read it." Gedcom files are electronic versions of family trees that can be read by any type of family tree software.

Raymond wrote back,

"Cousin Doug,

"Yes, no problem with the GEDCOM file, although it came in the body of the e-mail, instead of as an attachment like the other files. Probably a setting in you e-mail program that does that with text files, but no problem for me.

"OK, I have pasted below all that I have on your ancestry. Most of my sources are secondary and the ancestry of George Maris (b. 1596) is purely speculative at this time, so please keep that in mind.

"In the information you sent, you list the father of Madeline Laurnell Cooper as Edward Conlon. Can you tell me why their surnames aren't the same?

"Thanks again!"

"He never married her," I answered. This was getting personal.

"But he was the father of Madeline?" Raymond asked.

"Right, she is also my mother (deceased)."

"Cousin Doug,

"Yes, I see that she died when you were only 4. That must have been rough. My mother died when I was 12."

I didn't respond.

Was I starting to notice a pattern here? Was there something these genealogy fanatics had in common? Some desire to fit into the world, and connect to the greater global cosmic community? Were they trying to repair or redo their own family losses and short comings? Was this internet-based genealogy world really a lonely hearts club for parentally deprived adults who never grew up?

A few months later I got the following email.

"My name is Linda Conroy and I believe I have a Bible that belonged to Madeline Ella Rockey and her sister, Mary Gracia Rockey.

"The Bible has both names written in it with Madeline's name being associated with Charleston, West Virginia and Mary's name with Pennsylvania. Mary spelled her middle name as "Gracia" and not "Grace." It appears to have been a bible that was used for study and has various 1880's dates written on the pages along with notes. It also contains a lock of hair.

"I have had this in my possession for the past ten years. It was found in a crate that had been stored on a Colorado mountain property belonging to my grandmother. Her name was Lalah M Hurliman, and she was from Charleston, W.V. It seems the Bible was brought to Colorado around the early 1900's. These crates, among many other items, were stored in a barn for over 80 years and had never been reopened until about ten years ago when we moved my grandmother back to Denver. I was given all the books found in the barn and for many years thought the Bible belonged to some relative of my grandmothers.

"I have recently brought out my genealogy materials and did some research on the Rockey name. I did not find any connections to my family, so I decided to find someone that may be interested in having the Bible. .

"I wish I knew why my grandmother had this Bible in her possession. She was born in Charleston, W.V., in 1900, to Charles B. and Helen V. Hurliman. Helen was also born in Charleston in 1861 as Helen Virginia Mays. Charles B. was born in Switzerland in 1855, and came to America in 1870. As far as I can tell, there is no connection to Rockey.

"I would be very happy to send you the Bible if you are interested. I found you while searching Rootsweb and went to your web page. It seems that Madeline is your great-grandmother, so I felt it would be appropriate to offer the Bible to you in hopes you may want it or know someone in the family who would enjoy having it. Please feel free to contact me any time."

Madeline Ella Rockey, my grandmother Marian Bay Bremner's mother, was the daughter of Charlotte White Simcox and Thomas Jefferson Rockey. Born in 1873 in Lock Haven, Clinton County, Pennsylvania, her family had moved to Charleston, West Virginia, and later Bellingham, Washington. She is depicted in a picture earlier in this book. I thanked Linda and asked her to send the Bible.

I got the Bible a few days later in the mail.

The Bible was marked with little cryptic notes and clippings. I realized I had gained a window into the life of my great-grandmother, a woman I had never met, and about whom I knew essentially nothing.

Written in a fine hand in pencil on the inside cover were the names "Ella Rockey, Charleston, West Virginia" and "Mary Gracia Rockey, Williamsport, PA". Mary Rockey was Madeline Ella Rockey's sister. On another part of the inside cover, barely distinguishable, was "Madeline Ella Rockey, 6/25/89, commenced to read, 9/6/89, read to John 10/2/89."

The first few chapters of Genesis in the Bible were marked by dates, as if she were keeping track of her reading. Inserted into the Bible, at the beginning of Numbers, Chapter 32, which describes how The Lord made the Israelites wander in the desert for 40 years, was a lock of brown hair. At 1. Kings Chapter 21 and i. Kings Chapter 16 were pressed flowers. Did the verses have special meaning, or was this just a convenient place to press flowers? I figured it was probably the latter.

Inserted at Ezekiel Chapter 27, which was a lamentation for the city of Tyrus, was a clipping from a newspaper article entitled "A Presentation", which read as follows.

"One person in this city was made happy on Christmas by being the recipient of a number of handsome presents on that day. The pupils of Miss Eidson's select school took this opportunity of expressing their respect and esteem for their teacher by giving to her a number of beautiful and costly presents—among which was an elegantly bound volume of Shakespeare's complete works, a hymnal, together with a number of beautiful toilet articles. The presentation speech was made by Master Troxel, and was responded to in a neat and appropriate manner by Master Rockey—pupils of the school.

It was a happy event, and we doubt not the recipient appreciates the presents, not so much on account of their actual value, as for the love which influenced the pupils to give them. May both teacher and pupils live long to enjoy many recurrences of this happy season." On the flip side was part of an ad for "Hales [cutoff] Horehound and Tar" medicine "for cure of Colds, Influenza, Hoarseness, Difficulty Breathing, and all Affections of the Throat, Bronchial Tubes, and Lungs, leading to Consumption." A drawing of a bee hive amongst pine trees seemed to indicate the source of this wonderful medicine.

Inserted at Mark, Chapter 16, which was about the resurrection of Christ, was a clipping of a hymn.

"Sing (all standing)

Praise God from whom all blessings flow:
Praise him all creatures here below;
Praise him, above ye heavenly host,
Praise Father, Son, and Holy Ghost."

"BENEDICTION, BY THE PASTOR.

"Now unto him that is able to keep you from falling, and to present you faultless before the presence of his glory with exceeding joy, To the only God our Saviour, be glory and majesty, dominion and power, both now and ever."

Written inside the back cover of the bible was the word "Husband" underlined with Gen III, 6. and "Gold" underlined with Gen. II, 11. I eagerly turned to the verses noted, hoping to get some insight into my great-grandmother's thoughts on that most important subject for a young woman (she married five years later to Curtis Blackburn Bay).

Genesis Chapter 3, verse 6, states, "And when the woman saw that the tree was good for food, and that is was pleasant to the eyes, and a tree to be desired to make one wise, she took of the fruit thereof, and did eat, and gave also unto her husband with her, and he did eat."

This verse describes when Eve ate the forbidden fruit from the Tree of Knowledge of Good and Evil. Why did Madeline make a note of this verse under the title "husband"? Was she some kind of misogynist? Or maybe she was just taking notes for her Bible study class.

Genesis, Chapter 2, verse 11, states, "The name of the first is Pison, that is it which compasseth the whole land of Havilah, where there is gold."

This passage talked about the first of four rivers that God made run out of the garden of Eden. OK, so maybe the note 'husband' just helped her remember the passage, and was not some kind of clue to her premarital musings on matrimony.

But now I was hooked. I don't have a lot of interest in organized religion, but the idea that I could learn more about the inner musings of my great-grandmother, from over a century ago, at the tender age of sixteen, considering the fact that the Bible was the primary vehicle for expression of intimate thoughts and emotions at the time, was pretty heady stuff.

I read on. Barely readable in cursive inside the back cover was written "Psalms XIX, Let the words of…" and the rest was unintelligible. I turned to Psalms, Chapter 19. I found, "Let the words of my mouth, and the meditation of my heart, be acceptable in thy sight, O Lord, my strength, and my redeemer." In the margin was written, "May 18-1889" and "Essay".

OK, maybe these passages were not of personal interest, but merely topics she had been assigned to write about for Bible study class.

On top of the page Chronicles II, Chapter 32, were the words "Read, Watch, Pray."

I followed up a note about "Esther, 8-9" written inside the back cover.

Next to Esther, Chapter 8, verse 9, a passage that didn't seem to have any spiritual or philosophical nuggets, was the notation, "Longest verse."

OK, was this some kind of Biblical trivial pursuit?

I looked at the Rockey Bible lying in my lap. Although it offered tantalizing clues, there wasn't that much tangible information.

I imagined Madeline Ella Rockey, a girl of 16, sitting in Charleston, West Virginia, reading her Bible as she prepared for Bible study class.

Sitting with Madeline's bible on my lap, I felt calmer.

Chapter 3

Ancestry.com, a subscription-based service started by members of the LDS church, has two million subscribers, and is growing daily. Ancestry has put millions of documents online, including eight billion names and 28,000 historical records. They have census records for all of the US from the past 200 years, birth, marriage and death records, and more. In May of 2007 they dumped all of the military records of all of the soldiers who fought in all of the US wars, 90 million of them, online.

As the nuclear family continues to disintegrate, Americans are going online to reach out to 3rd cousins they never knew existed, post messages on message boards about their great-great-grandfathers, and find tombstones that were previously covered in weeds and overgrowth in an abandoned cemetery.

Genealogy is now America's #1 hobby.

And it isn't only the Americans that are getting hooked. It wasn't enough for the company that owns ancestry.com to scarf up all of the other web sites dealing in the genealogy topic, including genealogy.com, myfamily.com, and rootsweb.com (the free family tree archive, where anyone can upload their tree or chat in their "surname" groups). They also expanded their franchise to other countries, including the United Kingdom (ancestry.co.uk), France (ancestry.fr), Italy (ancestry.it), Germany (ancestry.de), Canada (ancestry.ca) and Australia (ancestry.au).

Millions of documents are being put on line so that subscribers can sit in their kitchens and type away, rather than traipsing across the country in search of obscure church and governmental archives. The internet, with sites like ancestry.com, genealogy.com, and familysearch.com, are helping to fuel this growth.

Ancestry.com was scorned in the business community because they said that once people found out the information they wanted, they would cancel their subscription. Ancestry's response was that once people got hooked, they could never let go. They may find out about their immediate ancestors, but there was always that distant cousin.

Can you say addiction?

When I think of genealogy addiction, the first person that comes to mind is John Brebner. The Brebner/Bremner web site, www.brebner.com, is a free site maintained by John Brebner, dedicated to "Researching the Brebner and Bremner families worldwide since 1988." Brebner was a variation of the spelling of the name Bremner, pointing to common family ties to a group of people who originally came from the rural countryside near Aberdeen, Scotland, the home town of John Brebner. Although not a member of the LDS Church, as far as I know, John Brebner has taken on the incredible task of trying to identify everyone on the planet who descended from the original tribe of Brebner/Bremners in Aberdeenshire, and has now spread to every point in the globe. He has on his website over 400 family genealogies, all carefully researched and referenced, with tens of thousands of names.

John wrote on his web site: "My interest in family history was sparked when hand-written pages that my grandmother had compiled for me some thirty years earlier turned up during spring cleaning. The lure of being able to input that data into a computer and to output family ancestral charts was the spur to beginning research on the Brebner/Bremner families worldwide...My addiction [his own choice of words] to genealogy fits well with a passion for photography.

"On my travels both around Canada and visits to Scotland, my cameras are always at hand. In 1998 I began a series of gravestone photographs that accompany some of the many monumental transcriptions in these pages, as well as photographs of landmarks, farms and homes linked to the various individuals. The more information uncovered, the greater the scope of the project still ahead.

"When I started, I had no idea that I would be finding links to the various families on such a worldwide scale. The research, first limited to Aberdeen, then to the North-East of Scotland, has expanded to a worldwide search. Many of the early families emigrated to North America, Australia and South Africa. The research is very much ongoing, with various projects always in progress. With the growing popularity of the internet, the global BREBNER/BREMNER family is starting to emerge. I welcome all contacts, additions, corrections and speculation on the family groups. Please have a look at my research philosophy. If this is your first visit to my pages, please drop me an e-mail and let me know if I can help in your search for BREBNER/BREMNER ancestors."

I emailed John .

"Dear John,

"Pretty impressive web site. I must have communicated with you at some point or someone got my tree because I see I am on your web site. It looks like you must have talked to my grandfather, George, or great-grandfather, Archie, both now deceased. I have taken over from my grandfather as 'family historian'. I noticed that your John Bremner b 25 Dec 1833 in Rhynie, Scotland, doesn't have a date or place of death. He is actually a fascinating guy (my great-great-uncle) who farmed in Iowa, and then abandoned his family. He later ended up in Alaska, when it was Russian Territory, lived with an Indian squaw, and had kids. When the first Americans arrived in Alaska, he served as a scout for a US expedition that explored previous uncharted territory, and was finally killed by the Indians. There are several geographical places named after him, including the John River, which flows into the Yukon, the Bremner River (where he wintered and wrote a diary) that flows into the Copper River, and the town of Bremner. There is also a World Heritage Site, the John Bremner Mining Area.

You can read about it at www.bremnerhistory.com or in the book *Sourdough Sagas*. You might want to look at the trees on my site, or I can send you my gedcom file (the one on the site is not totally updated). I see there are some dates you could fill in. There are also autobiographies going back five generations.

"Doug Bremner

"(James Douglas Bremner II, grandson of George Archibald Bremner II, From Lynden WA)."

John responded,

"Hi Doug,

"Many thanks for the information. I'm presently in Aberdeen and will have a more detailed look at your data when I return to Canada next week. As I recall, there is a large contingent of Alaskan-Scottish Bremners that I did try to connect to an existing Bremner, and it sounds as if your John must be that link. All fascinating stuff!

"Yes, I'd love to have an updated gedcom!

"Best wishes,

"John."

He added a link to my site and gave special mention to the diary of John Bremner, which I had transcribed on the site. John Bremner was the brother of my great-great-grandfather, James Bremner, an emigrant from Scotland. He later married Abigail Clark Freeman, a woman from Cape Cod whom he has corresponded with during the time he was a soldier for the Union Army in the Civil War. After they moved to the Washington Territory and carved out a home in the wilderness, he was kicked in the head by a horse, and died in 1887. Probably disgusted with her life on the farm, Abigail left for Powell River, British Columbia, Canada, where she died in 1915.

The descendants of John Bremner in Alaska were Native Americans. My grandfather had traveled there 50 years ago, and I remember a photo of him taken with them. They looked remarkably alike, apart from the fact that he was Anglo and they were Indian.

Shortly after setting up my bremnerhistory.com website I got the following email:

"Hello,

"My name is Chris Smith and my family is very close with the Bremners, the descendants of John Bremner II, here in Alaska. The Bremners do not live in Bremner or Chitina anymore, they moved to Yakutat a little over a hundred years ago (half of the town are Bremners). I have directed Amanda Bremner to your website, and she was floored. She is the great-great-great-granddaughter of John Bremner II. I am an anthropology major at the University of Alaska, Anchorage, and have been researching the Native and Scottish history of the Bremners for years. My father's best friend is Bertram Bremner, the son of John Bremner the 4th. Amanda and I are totally thrilled by your site. She had no idea other Bremner lines existed that are related to her. There are several books that chronicle the Bremner family in Alaska that are very good. These are: Under Mount St. Elias, by Frederica de Laguna, Haa Aani: Our Land by Walter Goldschmidt, available from the Sealaska Heritage website and Celebration 2000, also available from Sealaska. The St. Elias Books run about $300- $600.00 a set, but the Celebration 2000 offers an abridged version that includes the Bremners for about $20.00

"Amanda is going to a family dinner to tell everyone, so don't be surprised if you are flooded from Alaskan Bremners emailing you. Thanks so much for the site, this is great. Amanda is one of the last Bremners of this generation (There are lots of them, but they are mostly elderly) to bear the name, and my mother posed an amusing question several months ago, which you may also find amusing: If you and Amanda get married, would you take her last name? The answer was yes.

"Aatlein Gunalcheesh! (Thank you very much in Tlingit Language).

"Christopher Smith."

I responded as follows:

"Dear Chris,

"Thanks for the touching email, sorry for the delay in reply but I had stopped reading mail from this address because I never got any email, but then someone contacted me at another address and offered to send a lost family bible, so I figured I should take a look.

"I'm glad that the Alaska Bremners liked the web site. Are they Tshimshian? It is actually the contents of a book I wrote about 20 years ago. I since have been updating the genealogy and so on.

"I definitely will check out the books you mentioned. I have always been interested in Native cultures and art. Most of the Bremners of my family are in Western Washington, where I grew up. My grandfather, George A Bremner II, grew up on the Nooksack land and later reservation which is just south of the Canadian border, where James Bremner (brother of John) homesteaded. He visited the descendants of John Bremner about 40 years ago, I think one of them was named John Bremner, and had a picture taken with them that I saw a long time ago.

"I am happily married, but there are several unmarried Bremner males in their 20s, my nephew Joseph in Colorado, and some cousins in Washington and Oregon.

"I gave a lecture in Alaska last year where I threw in some slides about John Bremner just for the heck of it, and some Native people were in the audience, but they had never heard of any Native Bremners.

"If someone sends me the genealogy information, I can update rootsweb."

Christopher Smith replied:

"Hi Doug,

"It's really funny that you said that about John Bremner, because that is my "Uncle" Bert Bremner's (My dad's best friend and hunting partner) father and he told me that some Bremners showed up in Yakutat about forty years ago, and said that they looked just like his dad, except Caucasoid, and that was the last he had heard of them. He told me this after I directed him to your site. LOL. The Bremners are Tlingit, not Tsimshian (Who are looked down on by Tlingit people, as the Tsimshian were their slaves up until the 1860's) and are special in that there are two clans unique to their family: The Kwaashki'kwaan and Galyax Kaagwaantaan. Basically, they have two clans that are unique to their family based on the migration they made from the Copper River valley to Yakutat.

"With that said, I am unsure how to present this information, but Amanda's little brother, Nathan, had Down Syndrome and was diagnosed with Leukemia which he battled for a few months with in Seattle, until he passed away on July 4th (a week ago). There is a patient website http://www.thestatus.com/ where you can see family pictures and leave a note, if you are interested.

"There are family pictures and all of the Bremners here in Alaska are deeply grieved right now, but I thought I would share it with you.

Gunalcheesh (Tlingit thanks)

"Christopher Smith"

I did log on to the website. This was the last male Bremner from Alaska, in other words the end of the Alaskan Bremner line, who had died in Seattle. I followed the links to several sites describing how his totem animal was the Bear, and the Totem Pole carved in his honor in Alaska. Obviously he was well loved. But I couldn't get away from the fact that the Bremner line was done for in Alaska.

I asked Christopher Smith to forward information about some of the Alaskan Bremners so I could fill out the family tree, but he didn't respond.

I logged on to ancestry.com to see if I could find any evidence of the descendants of John Bremner. For the 1911 Census of "Kayak, Alaska" with "Chilcat-Indian Village" crossed out I found a John Bremner, whose "Tribe and Clan" was listed as "unknown", born in Alaska, mother born in Alaska, and birthplace of father unknown. Wife was Kulchtelch, Tribe and Clan,

Tlingit Yakutat, and sons Klairiche (7), Douch (4), Sheltuck (2), step sons Klashi, age 17, step daughter Kohaouhk, age 13, all Tribe and Clan Tlingit Yakutat.

A few weeks later I got the following email

"My grandmother was Susie Bremner, the granddaughter of John Bremner II. She had many brother and sisters including, John Bremner.

"Judy Ramos

"Yakutat, Alaska"

The Alaskan native missing link!

"Hi Judy," I wrote.

"I would appreciate any information you have about the Alaskan Bremners, like name, dates of birth and death, etc. I was contacted by a friend of an Amanda Bremner who works for the park service, and my grandfather (George Bremner) visited someone who I think was named John Bremner about 30 years ago. If you haven't seen it you should look at www.bremnerhistory.com where John Bremner II's diary is reprinted, and there is a history of his life.

"Doug Bremner (James Douglas Bremner II)"

She replied,

"I am guessing John Bremner, his son was born around 1877, he married Mary John's (born abound 1870). My grandmother Susie, was born in 1901. John Bremner and Mary died around 1918.

"Judy Ramos

51

"Yakutat, Alaska"

"What were your parents' names, year of birth, etc.," I wrote back. "We have a picture of two of your Bremner male relatives with my grandfather from 40 years ago; they were tall and thin with high cheek bones. They said "he looks just like us except he is an Anglo."

"My gram Susie's brother, John James Bremner was born 4/16/12 in Katella and died 2/28/2002 in Sitka. He had 12 kids. My gram Susie Bremner Abraham has 4 kids. My mother is Elaine Abraham. Sarah Bremner was born in 1910. I'll have to ask when Susie's Brother, George Bremner was born and died.

"Judy Ramos.

"Yakutat, Alaska."

"Do you know the name of your grandfather or the names of the parents of your grandmother?" I asked. I didn't get a reply for a couple of months.

"I've been busy with Christmas," she finally replied. "My grandmother Susie Bremner's brothers were Harry Bremner, George Bremner and John Bremner, her sister was Sarah Bremner Williams."

"Judy Ramos

"Yakutat, Alaska"

I forwarded her email to John Brebner and he wrote back.

"Hi Doug,

"I've been having a look at those Alaskan BREMNERS given the information that you had from Sue Ramos.

"I've attached what appears to be the family in the 1920 US census.

"Sara was living with Olaf ABRAHAM and her sister Susie; George and Jackson (who I suspect is John James) are with the JOHNSON family, and their relationship looks to be that of "nephew" to George. I wonder if Mary JOHNS should be Mary JOHNSON?

"Probably colder here in Ottawa right now than in Yakutat ... -25, so I'll be staying home and poking around the census data!

"Best wishes,

"John"

I emailed Judy Ramos.

"Were the parents of your grandmother Susie John Bremner and Mary Johns? Did the name Mary Johns come from you or is that something I had before? And what happened to the Indians that were living on the Copper River in 1884 when John Bremner II lived there?"

She replied with the following web link,

Tundratimeslocal.ilisgvik.cc/Obj342$1449* 187702

The link was to a web site that showed her, her mother and "gram" Susie in what looked like a traditional Native American ceremony in Alaska.

She wrote, "Here is a picture of my grandmother Susie Bremner Abraham, my mother Elaine and me. Taken probably in the late 1970's. My grandmother grew up in Katella, Alaska with her father John Bremner (probably the III) and Mary John's Bremner. I think Mary was married before.

"Judy Ramos

"Yakutat, Alaska"

I forwarded the emails to John Brebner.

"Hi Doug," he replied.

"Thanks for the additional information. I'll e-mail Christopher Smith and see if I can get some answers about those native names in that census that I sent earlier. I still have an Alaskan Bremner fragment at http://www.brebner.com/uploads/bre29587.pdf that must tie in with the family, although until I know some of the Tlingit name translations is a bit of a mystery. Still, it's all very interesting, and I love that story about continuing the Bremner name in Alaska.... surely your wife might understand the need, even the necessity, of continuing the line! A better excuse for straying from the confines of a Presbyterian marriage I have yet to hear! Seriously though, you really should take a trip up there and fill in some of those family history details.

"I wondered if I might add some of the photos you had on your site to my Brebner/Bremner photo database? If you had any other old photos, I think they would also be a great addition.

"Best wishes,

"John"

I did a Google search for Amanda Bremner and found her MySpace web site. The only way I could contact her was to set up my own MySpace account. Being married and not really of the

MySpace generation I felt a little funny doing so. All I put on the account was my name and picture. In my first and last MySpace contact I sent her an email.

"Hi Amanda," I wrote.

"I got your name a couple of years ago from someone named Chris Smith who responded to the webpage I had about Bremner history. I had posted the diary of John Bremner II who I think is your great-great-grandfather (he was the brother of my great-great-grandfather). I have had some information from people from Yakutat since then and wanted to see if I could learn more about the Bremners in Yakutat.

"Doug Bremner."

She replied,

"Doug,

"I'm not sure what kind of information you're looking for. As far as I know most of my Bremner relatives are in Yakutat, AK and Washington State. We've kind of spread out over the years, but still mainly reside on the North West coast. I did notice, however, a year or so ago when my family was in the Children's Hospital in North Seattle, that there was another family also named "Bremner", but we were not directly related. They were not white, though, as I would have expected. So I think there are more out there :)

"Nice to meet you, though. It's interesting that we share the same surname and are, however distantly, related.

"-Amanda"

I replied,

"I am interested in genealogy and tracking down the descendants of John Bremner and the other Bremners who came from Scotland, their names, birthdays and that sort of thing, e.g. who your parents are."

She replied,

"Ohhh, gotchya. Okay, well I'll have to get back to you. Not only will that take some research on my part, but I will have to ask permission. When I gather everything I will e-mail it to your bremnerhistory.com address."

Shortly after that I got the following email.

"Hi Cutie! I saw your picture on myspace.com! I am looking for the boy next door! Send me an email!"

It looked like the woman who sent the email was young enough to be my daughter.

That email kind of confirmed the weird nature of my reaching out to myspace.com to make my genealogy connections. I figured my wife wouldn't appreciate my socializing on myspace.com, so I made my account non-public.

Amanda Bremner never got back to me with her family tree. The Judy Ramos and Alaskan Bremner trail went cold.

However, I had extended my family tree.

At that point I had to ask myself, was I pushing things too far in my genealogy quest? Was this an invasion of privacy, or a legitimate quest? Wasn't it weird for me to be using internet programs designed to facilitate mating to get my genealogy data?

What was this genealogy thing all about anyway?

Chapter 4

ge·ne·al·o·gy(jn-l-j, -l-, jn-)

n. pl. ge·ne·al·o·gies

1. A record or table of the descent of a person, family, or group from an ancestor or ancestors; a family tree.

2. Direct descent from an ancestor; lineage or pedigree.

3. The study or investigation of ancestry and family histories.

This is the dictionary definition of genealogy. The derivation of the word literally means a written record (logos) of one's family (geneo).

I love to read about history, and one of my life-long projects has been reading the fourteen volumes of the *Cambridge Ancient History*. One of the things that I gleaned from those books is that the ancient Romans venerated their ancestors. The head of the family was called the *Pater familias*. He had special power and control over other members of the family. As the spouse of a Sicilian, I had encountered a similar phenomenon when my wife and I visited her family in her native Sicily. I was placed at the head of the table, and called the *capo di tavola*, or head of the table. With this honor, given to a visitor, came honors as the lead male.

The Romans also kept images of their ancestors in their homes that they would worship. What did this mean for them? And more important, what did it mean for the current crop of American genealogy addicts?

After a quick search on Wikipedia and freedictionary.com, I discovered that a number of cultures have venerated their ancestors, including the ancient Romans and Greeks. Veneration of the spirits of one's ancestors is common in China and other Asian countries.

Known in English as "Ancestor Worship," this practice is not really a religion, but rather a belief that deceased family members have a continued existence, take an interest in the affairs of the world, and possess the ability to influence the fortune of the living.

Some people believe that continued care for the dead is required for their well being. Others think that devotion to dead ancestors is a matter of duty, regardless of what effects may come from the performance of that duty.

Some people just do it, and they don't know why.

Chapter 5

I kept trying to find the names of my mother's parents. I used various web sites, like www.rootsweb.com, without any luck.

It seemed that Alice Pauline Woods and Edward Conlon never existed.

In my search for my mother, I was stuck.

I also had doubts about whether the parents of my mother wanted to be contacted.

I knew she was born out of wedlock, and back in those days her birth would have been a source of shame.

Even if her mother was still alive, she might still want things kept secret.

My grandmother might have wished that I never came into existence in the first place, let alone come back years later as the bastard emerging from the woodshed.

I was having serious doubts.

Should I just stop this?

Chapter 6

Madeline Lucile Cooney Cooper and Lyndle Ross Cooper were school teachers who moved from one small wheat farming town in Eastern Washington State to another over the course of the 1930s and 1940s. Lyndle was born and raised in Illinois, and Madeline in a town in Eastern Oregon called Dallas.

Madeline was one of thirteen children born to a hard drinking migrant farm laborer and a long-suffering woman named Lulu, who was tricked into giving up her kids for adoption after she got sick and her derelict husband was nowhere to be found. Madeline was sent off to live with strangers when she was eight years old, and never saw her mother again. When they grew up, the kids tried to find each other, and found all but one.

Madeline's own first child was born in 1931 in Wenatchee, Washington. Wenatchee is known as the apple growing capital of the world. They planned to name the child Madeline Laurnell. Madeline Cooper was in labor for over ten hours. They called the doctor repeatedly, but he was late in arriving. By the time he got there, the baby was dead.

Madeline Cooney Cooper became depressed after the death of her child. The couple moved to Four Lakes, Washington, a wheat farming community just west of Spokane, where they started over teaching in the local school. She arranged to adopt a baby. She gave the baby the same name as her dead child, Madeline Laurnell Cooper, although she went by the name of

Laurnell, a conglomeration of the names of two of her friends, Laurell and Nell.

One year later they had a biological child, that they named Vinnie. That was their only other child. A few years later, they moved to Reardan, another wheat farming town thirty miles west of Spokane, and once again got jobs teaching at the local school.

Lyndle Ross Cooper died before I was born. The only thing I remember about Madeline Cooney Cooper is her sending a box of presents at Christmas time when I was four years old. My mother died a few months later. I never saw them again.

I have a clear memory of sitting in the garden one summer day when I was a little four-year-old boy, in our home on Fishtrap Creek, outside of Olympia, Washington. A bee was buzzing around me. Although I had an extreme childish fear, I thought that if I stayed very still it would not notice me and sting me. If I sat still enough, I would become invisible.

That was shortly before her death.

There were a lot of stories about my mother that ran in the family.

She had an olive skin complexion and black hair. That didn't fit with the usual English and Scandinavian backgrounds of most of the people from Eastern Washington. My father said that she was a Laplander, or a 'Black Irish'.

Here she is holding my sister, Anne, in Wounded Knee, South Dakota, in about 1959. My father was working as a doctor there in the Public Health Service.

My father felt that her adoptive parents knew the identity of her real parents, but didn't want to tell anyone. He said that Madeline Cooney Cooper said that if people knew the truth it would be 'too upsetting'.

Madeline Cooney Cooper died in 1992. A couple of years after her death, her biological daughter and my mother's step-sister, Vinnie, contacted my sister, Lynn. She made the drive from Gresham, Oregon, to Long Beach, Washington, where my sister lives. Long Beach is a town on a long spit of sand on the Washington Coast, where it rains more often than not, and where the economy is based on shoveling clams and a dying salmon fishing industry. My sister Anne (from Seattle) met them there in Long Beach.

Vinnie gave them a number of pictures and some family history. My sister Lynn wrote a letter with the results of that meeting which I filed away but didn't read carefully. I later learned that Vinnie's trip was stimulated by information she had learned about my mother on her mother's deathbed.

The issue of my paternity languished for the next decade. I became absorbed in my work and raising my own family, including Sabina, born in 1992, and Dylan, born in 1997, both in New Haven, Connecticut.

In 2000, we moved to Atlanta, Georgia, and jobs at Emory University. As part of some of the research I was doing I became an expert on the toxic effects of a drug for the treatment of acne, called Accutane, which had the unfortunate side effect of causing some people to become depressed and kills themselves. Rather than accept the results of my research, and give up their drug that was making them a billion dollars a year, the drug company decided to come after me instead. I wrote about that story in my book *The Goose That Laid the Golden Egg*, which was published in 2011.

During the course of that experience, something inside of me sort of snapped, and I asked myself, "Why am I holding back on learning about my family because I am worried about what people might think? Why shouldn't I learn about my family, because I want to know the information? Who cares what other people think?"

I read in *The New York Times* about a company called DNA Printgenomics that could analyze your DNA and tell you where your ancestors came from. I figured that since I knew nothing about where my mother came from it would be worth a try. I sent in a swab of my cheek, and for $300, got a complete DNA analysis.

At the same time, I started looking on the internet for genealogists who could help me with my quest. I found Donna Potter, a genealogist from Spokane, WA, on the internet.

I wrote the following email:

"Dear Donna,

"I have some genealogical research I would like done in Spokane, and wondered if you are available to do that, and if so, what would be the charge."

I later got the following response from a man named Charles Hansen:

"Doug, Donna passed this on to me, I do research for a donation to Eastern Washington Genealogical Society, and my costs (copies and postage). Who are you looking for?"

I was excited. I responded,

"Dear Charles,

"Thanks for your help. Alice Pauline Woods had a child in Spokane on Feb 23, 1932, who was adopted by Lyndle Cooper of Four Lakes WA. The adoption was arranged by the Washington Children's' Home Society [I later learned this wasn't true], Robert B. Ralls State Superintendent, 601 Home Savings Building, Seattle. Adoption was performed by Chas H Leavy, Judge, for Jane Doe Woods, May 20, 1932 in Superior Court of WA, for the County of Spokane. Attorney was H. Earl Haris. Father of the baby listed on the birth certificate as Edward Conlon, E 2123 Central Ave., Employee of Dessert Hotel, born in 1906 (Spokane? died in 81 out of state?). Doctor was JF Hall MD, 601 Fernwell Bldg. Address of Alice Woods, listed as N 2618 Altamont (although this could have been a birthing home) age 19, at time of childbirth. Birthing mother Mrs. Edith Gilbert.

Charles quickly found out that Edward Conlon had used his step-father's last name on the birth certificate, and that his real name was Edward Ehrlich. He found an Alice Woods who was 18 years old and listed on the 1930 census in Seattle as "wife" underneath William Woods, age 23, and "head" of the household. The census stated that Alice was born in Canada, "E" (for English speaking), with her father born in Canada and her mother in Washington.

William Woods was listed as a machinist at an auto plant in Seattle, who was born in North Carolina, and whose parents were born in the "U.S." Also listed was Myra J. Woods, daughter, age two months, Fred A. Rosenberg, 37, father-in-law (i.e., Alice's father), whose occupation was electrician, Flora Rosenberg, 37, mother in law, and Fred, age 16, brother-in-law (Alice's brother). The date of immigration from Canada to the US was 1914. Charles felt it was a likely match, and he couldn't find any other Alice Woods anywhere else.

Since Alice was eighteen in 1930, that would make her 94 in 2006. In other words, she could still be alive. What a thought!

I did a quick search on the internet for the Ehrlich name, and got a list of rabbis. Rosenberg was an obvious Jewish name as well. At that time I got the results of my DNA analysis. It showed that I was 95% European, and 4% Sub-Saharan African; a breakdown of the European part showed that I was 44% Northern European, 34% Middle Eastern, 22% Southeastern European, 0% South Asian.

What a surprise! I had no idea where the Sub-Saharan African part came from, but that meant that I had a black ancestor somewhere about five generations back. My father's family was all early American settlers living on the frontier, with no hint of an exposure to Jews. Since my mother came from small towns in Eastern Washington, I had never considered the possibility that she could be Jewish.

I looked up the British Columbia Birth Registration online, assuming that the Rosenbergs had emigrated from Vancouver, which is the closest large city to Seattle. I found a Frederick A. Rosenberg, born April 19, 1892, in Vancouver. The name and year of birth matched exactly. A search of the Social Security Death Index showed a Frederick A. Rosenberg with the same birthdate had obtained his social security number in Washington State and died in Coeur D'Alene, Idaho, in December of 1970. I sent off letters to the King County Department of Vital Records asking for information about Myra J. Woods, and for a marriage certificate for William and Alice Woods.

I next turned my attention to Fred Rosenberg, Jr. A search of the Social Security Death Index showed a Fred Page Rosenberg born in Canada on July 26, 1913, who died in Seattle on May 19, 1986. I wrote to the King County Department of Vital Records for a copy of his death certificate.

Meanwhile, I looked up the Rosenbergs on www.rootsweb.com. Someone had Fred Rosenberg, Sr., on their family tree as someone married to Flora Hurn. Flora Hurn was the daughter of a pioneer family near Rochester, Washington, a small town near Olympia, the town where I grew up. I emailed the person who had him on her family tree. She couldn't tell me much, but recommended I talk to a Hurn descendant, named Ted Hurn. He was in his 80s and living in Tacoma, Washington.

I called up Ted Hurn. "I remember Fred and Flora Rosenberg," he said. "We gave them a ride from Sunnyside, Washington, to Seattle after a family visit. That was over fifty years ago."

"What do you remember about them?" I asked.

"Fred worked at Continental Can in Seattle."

"Did he mention a daughter Alice?"

"He talked all the time about his son; I don't remember him talking about a daughter."

I thought that was strange. Maybe more evidence that something had gone wrong that caused the family to disown Alice, like an out of wedlock birth.

I searched on ancestry.com for evidence of the death of Alice Woods or William Woods, and could find nothing. Maybe she was still alive? Or she could have remarried, changing her name and making it very difficult to trace. I paid for a search on USSearch.com for all Alice Woods in the country who were born in 1912, plus or minus a year. I got a list of about 13. I picked out two as the most likely candidates, both of them 94 years old, one living in Miami, the other in Ft Lauderdale, Florida. For an extra charge, USSearch gave me a detailed list of information about the two Alice candidates, including their addresses for the past twenty years, their criminal history (none, thankfully), the value of their property, and an aerial view of their homes.

I wrote a form letter to the thirteen Alice candidates. "Dear Alice," I wrote. "I am doing research on my family and want to see if we might be related. Have you ever lived in Spokane, Washington?" I gave them a checkbox for yes or no and a stamped self addressed envelope.

I read in one of my books about genealogy that the next of kin is often listed on original death certificates, and that getting the original was a great way to extend your family tree. I waited anxiously for the death certificate of Fred Rosenberg, Jr.

As I looked for the real Alice Woods, I also looked for information on my grandfather, Edward Joseph Ehrlich, on the message boards of www.rootsweb.com. I found a woman named Denise Ehrlich who was looking for information on an Edward Ehrlich who came from Spokane, Washington. I emailed her, but got no response.

Since the posting was several years old, maybe I was trying to contact her through a defunct email address? I googled her name, and found a Denise Ehrlich who worked for a wine distributor. I was able to get another email address through the web site for her current employer.

"Are you related to a man named Edward Ehrlich from Spokane, Washington?" I tentatively emailed. I didn't hear back right away.

I emailed my sister, Anne.

"I have two good candidates for our grandmother, Alice Rosenberg. I'm thinking about giving her a call. I don't know if she wants to talk to us, though. She's probably married, and her husband probably wouldn't be excited about us intruding in her life."

"Maybe she's just a kind old lady that would like to talk to somebody," my sister replied.

That was a good way to think about it, I thought.

I didn't get any response to my mailings. I thought that maybe Alice got spooked by the Spokane reference. I really wanted to know, one way or another, so I decided to give the two Alice candidates a call.

As I picked up the phone to call, my palms were sweating. I felt like I did when I was seventeen-years-old and called up girls to ask them out for a date. The line was busy. I called again in a half hour. Still busy.

Denise Ehrlich wrote back

"Yes— My grandfather was Edward Joseph Ehrlich, who was married to Katherine Leonard; both of Spokane, WA.

"Are we related?

Chapter 7

In 1823, a farm boy named Joseph Smith claimed that the Angel Moroni appeared in front of him as he was walking through the forest in Upstate New York.

The Angel Moroni led him to a set of inscribed golden plates. The plates contained the Book of Mormon, which tells about how the lost tribe of Israel came to America 2,000 years ago. Commanded by God, they inscribed the plates to record their religion and genealogies. In addition to the Angel Moroni, Joseph Smith was visited by God and Jesus Christ, who told him that the teachings of Jesus had been corrupted and that he was to found a new church with the purified teachings of Jesus. This new church was comprised of "Latter Day Saints," or the LDS Church, more commonly known as the Mormons, who alone held the pure and undistilled teachings of the true church.

In 1836, Joseph Smith announced that the prophet Elijah had appeared to him and granted the priesthood of the LDS Church the ability to "seal" families together for eternity, including dead ancestors, and even the entire mass of dead humanity. In 1842, the prophet introduced the temple ordinances in Nauvoo, Illinois, including the ability of church members to act as proxies for deceased persons, baptize them, and "seal" them into family clans that will be reunited in Heaven. He said, "we redeem our dead, and connect ourselves with our fathers which are in heaven, and seal up our dead to come forth in the first resurrection...[we] seal those who dwell on earth to those who dwell in heaven"... this sealing work "fulfills the mission of Elijah". Dead ancestors introduced to the church in temple ceremonies are believed to have the capacity to accept or reject their introduction to the church in the spiritual world.
http://www.lightplanet.com/mormons/temples/sal vation_dead.html

However, since the Church has only been around since 1832, what were they to do about family members born before that time? The solution was to baptize them after the fact, so that they could join the other family members in the hereafter.

In the 1840s, Brigham Young, the Mormon pioneer who led the way to Utah after Smith's murder in 1844, wrote about "the perfect mania" (his choice of words) that possessed some of his followers as they started "to get up printed records of their ancestors."

The mania continues to this day.

Chapter 8

I stared at the computer screen. I was faced with the possibility that I was corresponding via email with someone with whom I actually shared a common grandfather.

That was pretty heady.

She had just asked me if we were related.

The details were related to Edward Joseph Ehrlich.

"Did his mother marry someone named Conlon?"

She answered,

"Yes, I have been trying to find Conlon relatives. Edward's brother was Hal Conlon. I've also been trying to find his mother's relatives in Canada. Her name was Emma Powers. How did you find me?"

I responded, "My mother (now deceased) was put up for adoption at birth. I had the adoption records opened ten years ago. The records stated that my mother was born out of wedlock. The mother was listed as Alice Pauline Woods and the father as Edward Conlon, employee of the Dessert Hotel. I was unable to trace either person through the internet, even though I have a large list on my father's side who are all English or Northern European. Last week I hired a genealogist who told me that Edward Conlon also listed his name as Ehrlich, and that his step-father was named Conlon. He also found an Alice Woods living with A. E. Woods. The census listed in-laws living in the same household named Rosenberg. I hadn't been able to trace either, because I had their names wrong.

"I also got my DNA tested, and was shocked (as are my three siblings) that genetically I am almost half Jewish, as far as I can tell. Forty-four percent Northern European, thirty three percent Middle Eastern, and twenty two percent Southern European. None of my father's side ever went anywhere near the Mediterranean. I assume that Jewish people have some Southern European genes (centered in Greece and Turkey). I'm also four percent African, genetically. You might want to get yourself checked. You can get a kit at www.ancestrybydna.com.

"You can find Edward Conlon by clicking on surnames in www.bremnerhistory.com.

"Emma and Thomas Conlon lived at E 2123 Central until they died in 1952 and 1962.

"My mother's adoptive parents told her that she looked dark because she was a Laplander. It looks to me like she is more Jewish or mixed Jewish-Italian or something like that. If I am correct, her maternal grandmother was Irish. So that means technically I am not Jewish? I am still getting over the shock of all of this.

"Hope I am not springing any unwelcome news on you, but since you responded, I figured you might be interested.

"You can read about my siblings at:

"Steve Bremner (CO) http://cloud.prohosting.com/~mtnclmbr/crestone.htm.

"Anne Bremner (Seattle)
www.abremner.com.

"My other sister is Lynn Dickerson, who lives in Long Beach, WA.

"I guess they are your cousins, too.

"I am a physician at Emory University in Atlanta. I am married and have two kids.

"Right now, I'm actually at the National Archives in Atlanta, tracing all this stuff on the free version of ancestry.com."

She wrote back

"Hi Doug,

"Very interesting stuff! I left a message a little while ago for you at the home number you provided. I can be reached at any of the numbers listed below. I never knew Edward had used the name Conlon. The story I heard was that Thomas Conlon adopted the step-sons but Edward chose to keep his paternal name and Hal used his adopted name. "Apparently, Hal and Edward stayed in touch through the 50's. I have some Christmas snapshots of Hal and his family from 1955.

"I had always been told we were related to a famous attorney, named Jake Ehrlich. That particular line of Ehrlichs is Jewish – My grandfather did not talk about his past much. Jake was also the name of Edward's natural father. I have not been able to find a link between these two branches of Ehrlichs. Edward was a devout Catholic and always saw himself as Irish. He married a full blooded Irish gal named Katherine Leonard. I have not been able to find any of the Leonard clan, although I know they are in California and Spokane. When I was very young I came across a newspaper clipping in an old book in our Los Angeles home (I grew up in the house my father grew up in). The clipping talked about an Edward Ehrlich being a long lost heir, and how a reporter happened to find him working as a theatre attendant, and mentioned the only thing he had from his father was a watch with the father's name engraved in it. When I asked about the clipping, it was brushed aside, and I never really got any answers. My mother later told me my grandfather Ehrlich's life seemed to have lots of secrets nobody wanted to talk about.

"I know my father has a half-brother he never met. My mother told me my Grandfather's first wife died at a very young age, and the son from that marriage was later disowned due to his bad character. I have no idea if any of that is true. My brother tells me he was at my parents' house when they got a phone call from the half-brother's wife saying he had passed away. That had to have been in the last 10 or 15 years. I had no idea he had fathered another child earlier, or that he had ever gone by the name Edward Conlon. I found a 1930 census record where he is listed as a step-son in the Conlon household and his name is incorrectly spelled Erlich.

"I may look into the genetic testing link you sent, but I have to tell you I am not surprised at all by the Jewish descendancy you discovered. As for your mother's dark coloring, it's not really that indicative. Edward had sandy hair and blue eyes. His Irish wife. Katherine, had very dark hair, fair skin and brown eyes. My father has the same dark hair and brown eyes as his Irish mother, and his sister has blonde hair and blue eyes. My brother is also dark haired and brown eyed. I am dark haired, with hazel eyes and very fair skin. We always said we were "black Irish."

"I am attaching some pictures for you, and I look forward to hearing from you again.

"Cheers!

"Denise Ehrlich."

She gave me her number, and I gave her a ring. I was very excited. This was the first tangible connection with someone related to my mother.

"I have guests coming over in a couple of hours and I can't talk to you right now," she said. "But I will call you back, I promise."

I called up Alice Rosenberg, of Miami Ft. Lauderdale, Florida. The line was busy.

The next day Denise Ehrlich called me back. We discovered that we had the same grandfather, Edward Joseph Ehrlich, born July 16, 1905 in Spokane, Washington, to Jacob Ehrlich and Emma Powers. She had been looking for information about him as well, as he had always been secretive about his past, and she was suspicious that there was more about the family history that she didn't know about. I told her about my efforts to find Alice Rosenberg. She emailed me a photograph of Edward. He was standing in someone's yard, about 25 years old, hands in his pockets, with a cocky grin. I could sort of imagine a family resemblance.

I emailed her back

"I think I look like Edward, especially the nose and the sunken eyes. You look a little like my sister Lynn.

"I had another thought. Since I am 34% Middle Eastern, then my mother would have had to be 75% Jewish at least, and if Alice Woods was really Alice Rosenberg, whose mother was pure Irish, then Emma Powers would have had to have been at least half Jewish."

She wrote back

"You definitely look like Edward! Edward's mother, Emma Powers, should be English/Irish, but maybe she had a mixed background and that is why she married Ed's father, Jake Ehrlich, to begin with. Alice Woods (Rosenberg) would appear to be where the remaining Middle

Eastern percentage comes from in your genetic profile.

"Edward married Katherine Leonard, who was 100% Irish, but of course, that has no bearing on your genetic make-up.

"The older picture is my aunt. I have not been able to get her to post any more recent pictures. I think she also looks like Edward in the eye area. My Dad and my brother both have more sunken eyes. It's hard to tell from my picture below, but mine are somewhere in between my Dad's and my Mom's eyes.

"I'm trying to figure out how to get the tree I am working on at Ancestry.com online linked to my family webpage. I've downloaded Family Tree Maker in the meantime – this will probably distract me from work for a while.

"I tried to reach Fern Ehrlich [wife of the deceased Edward Ehrlich II] yesterday, but both phone numbers I found were disconnected. I hope she is still living somewhere. I have not been able to find her in the social security death index yet. Any luck getting in touch with Alice?

"Denise Ehrlich"

I wrote back,

"Her phone is always busy. She must be leaving it off the hook because she knows her grand kids are after her. I also paid for a people search for what I assume is the same person. She is the only traceable 92 year old Alice Rosenberg alive. I'm going to get the mitochondrial DNA test, because if it comes back as the Irish Eve that would be good evidence for it being Alice Rosenberg."

Mitochondria are located in all of the cells of the body, and act as little power stations for the cells. By some fluke of nature, they have their own DNA, separate from the cell's main DNA, that doesn't seem to serve any useful purpose.

However, they do serve a handy purpose for genealogists, because an intact, unchanged copy of the mitochondrial DNA from our mothers. Mutations occur only every several thousand years. About twelve different original forms of mitochondrial DNA, or "haplotypes," have been identified. Based on how common they are in different parts of the world, there are some guesses about where the original "Eves" that started these matrilineal lines came from. Some of the lines of the Eves have of course gone extinct in the past, as the last in the long line of women was not able to bear a daughter to carry on the line.

About twelve original "Eves" have been identified, from whom all people on the planet have descended in an unbroken line of matrilineal descent. Based on who your "Eve" is, you can figure out where your mother and her mother's mother came from, and so on. Since Judaism is passed on through mothers, my mitochondrial DNA test would tell me if I were a "real Jew". I eagerly sent off a swab of my cheek in the mail for analysis, in exchange for a small fee.

I called Alice Rosenberg from Ft. Lauderdale. An elderly woman with a kind sounding voice answered the phone.

"There was an Alice Rosenberg who lived in our retirement complex," she said. "I think she moved to Kansas a couple of years ago."

I thanked her and dialed the other Alice Rosenberg number.

An elderly man answered the phone. He sounded like someone who was originally from New York, possibly Jewish.

"I'm doing research on my family tree and I want to see if we might be related?" I asked. I felt like a telephone solicitor.

"I don't want any of that!" the man shouted at me.

"Could you just let me know if Alice Rosenberg lives there?"

"I don't think you're at the right place. But don't call me anymore!" he shouted, and hung up the phone.

I couldn't be entirely sure, but I had the feeling that this wasn't the right Alice. For one thing, I couldn't imagine someone of my flesh and blood living with such an awful man.

Denise Ehrlich emailed me back.

"I don't understand where you're getting the Irish part from Alice Rosenberg? Do you think Alice's mother was part Irish? I did not get that from anything we looked at yesterday. From what I saw, Alice's only connection to anything Irish would have been her marriage to W. E. Woods, which of course would have no bearing on your genetic make-up. Did you find Alice's mother's maiden name somewhere?"

"Carroll - Asher family tree. You can find it by going to the family trees in ancestry.com and typing in Fred A Rosenberg. It lists his wife as Flora Irene Hurn, which matches the census listing of his household. Their kids are not listed. Both her parents were born in Ireland, and she was born in Rochester. WA (near Olympia) making her an early pioneer."

"How crazy is that?! What are all these Irish girls doing marrying Jewish men? It seems a little unusual for the time don't you think? Unless of course the men were converted?"

I replied, "Back then the Irish were considered to be at the same level as farm animals, so that was probably the only women they could get to go out with them."

"I found two phone numbers for Alice Rosenberg. Age 92, in Florida. One was a nice woman who remembered someone by that name who moved to Kansas. The other was a guy who acted strange and when I called him back he yelled at me. He was a very bad man. He sounded like he was old and didn't get out much. I feel kind of strange talking to these old Jewish people from Florida. Anyway my sister is a lawyer, and they have all kinds of dirty tactics for tracking people down, so I'm going to get her on it. She's a commentator on TV for legal issues a lot so she's mainly motivated to prove that she's related to Perry Mason and Jewish."

The real name of the person the TV lawyer Perry Mason as based on was Jacob Ehrlich, the same name of the father of Edward Joseph Ehrlich, as we had discovered. The lawyer Ehrlich lived in San Francisco in the 40s and made a number for himself successfully defended celebrities against charges of murder and other crimes.

"Did you get the documents I scanned from the obituaries of the Conlons?" I asked. "Did they provide any new information on people you didn't know about? I noticed your rootsweb is not really updated. When you get your software for FTM you can do a save as--> gedcom and then go to rootsweb and go to edit your tree and then upload the gedcom."

"Doug"

"Hi Doug," she replied. "Sorry to hear about your run in with the mean guy. I did not receive the Conlon obits— please resend them— I think they might be helpful. I usually don't have any trouble receiving stuff at this address.

"I just removed the rootsweb file and I am re-entering all of the info in a new FTM file so I can upload it. I had been updating a tree on the Ancestry.com "OneWorld Tree." I thought everyone would have access through my family site, but that is not the case, and I can't even download it. I'll have to retype almost everything. It's tedious, but I'll get it done and then upload it again to rootsweb. I don't think I'll get it done in the next two weeks. I have lots of travel and meetings scheduled for the next ten to fifteen days.

"I like the idea of getting your sister involved in the investigation— she's probably heard of Jake Ehrlich (the famous lawyer). You can still find copies of his books. Maybe she can help with looking into old probate records. Here is a link to the website Jakes Sr's grandson set up: http://www.neverpleadguilty.com/

"Here is the grandson's website:
http://www.jakeehrlich.com/index.html

"Cheers!

"Denise Ehrlich."

Denise didn't have a close connection with the other relatives that were still living in Spokane, Washington. Denise told me that she had talked to a descendant of Jacob Ehrlich, the San Francisco lawyer, Jacob Ehrlich III, who was currently owned a company that manufactured jeans called "Jakies Jeans". I gave him a call and left him a voice mail detailing my questions about whether I was related to the original Jake Ehrlich, the lawyer from San Francisco.

Meanwhile I talked with someone at work who didn't know who her real father was. She was born to a Vietnam woman and an American soldier during the Vietnam War. Her mother moved with her when she was a baby to Indiana and remarried. She didn't tell her that her step-father wasn't her real father until she was a teenager.

"I have a picture of my real father," she gave me the name.

I felt adventurous.

"Why don't you let me use my search skills and see what I can find out," I said.

I went back to my computer and logged in to Intellius.com. I reasoned that someone who had fathered a child during the Vietnam War would have been born sometime between 1940 and 1950, making them 50–60 or so today. A search came up with 13 men with that description. I picked one that fit the description that was in Ohio. A search on the internet came up with a woman married to the man with the correct name. Her email was listed. I emailed her and asked if she was married to that person.

"Yes, why?" she responded.

"Was he living in Ohio in the 1970s?" I asked, hoping that I would flush out the response that he was in Vietnam during that time."

"No, why do you ask?"

"A friend of mine's mother is Vietnamese. Her father was a soldier. Was your husband in Vietnam?"

I didn't get a response.

After a few days I emailed her again.

"You shouldn't make such accusations, you can hurt people. But I don't think my husband is the one you're looking for."

Oops, I guess I messed up on that one, I thought.

While I was waiting for more information to come in about my mysterious grandmother, I went back to my long-term research project on my great-great-great-great-grandmother, Sarah Eleanor (Lee) Wilson. She was buried with her Bible, November 27, 1876, in Shelby County, Illinois. According to the family legend, in her Bible she wrote that she was the granddaughter of Richard Henry Lee, the man who moved that Virginia should separate from England at the time of the American Revolution, and a member of the Lee family that produced Robert E. Lee, the general who led the Confederate States in the American Civil War. Obviously there was a lot of history to find, not to mention a genealogical treasure trove to discover, if I could link her to the Lees, whose family tree is one of the best documented in America. However, the Lee genealogies I had looked up years ago did not mention her.

I had sent twenty on the problem, going to LDS family history libraries to do research, coming through microfilms and census data bases, with no luck. Sarah Eleanor Lee Wilson and her husband, Augustus Wilson, had apparently come out of nowhere, either somewhere in Virginia or Maryland, spent time in Lewis County, Kentucky, a place on the Ohio River just across from Indiana, where most of their children were born, then moved on to a farm in Shelby County Indiana where her husband died soon after they arrived.

On rootsweb I discovered a web page for Shelby County, where grave site information was listed. I emailed someone named Melinda Weaver on the list.

"Dear Melinda

"I was told that my ancestor, Sarah Eleanor (Lee) Wilson (aka Ellen Wilson), who died in 27 Nov 1874, was buried in Canaan cemetery, in Shelby County, but I cannot find it anywhere. They once lived in Moral Township, and also listed Fountaintown as a post office on the census. I have a number of other Wilson family members buried there, including Ruggle (Ruggal). Any help you can give is appreciated.

"Thanks, Doug Bremner"

I got this reply

"Doug,

"Caanon Cemetery is also known as Ruggels Cemetery. It is in Moral Township, in a field off of 1050 North. According to the book, it is overgrown with trees and weed and no longer cared for.

"The Ruggels buried there are:

"Amos, Albert, Silvester, Walter, Enoch, Ruth, John, Elizabeth, John W., Martha A., William, Thomas, William M., Abraham, Galveston, and John N.

"Wilsons:

"Augustus, Amelia, Jonathan (Rev.), Mary E, Louisa J., Jonathan, Sally A, Sally A (both have different dates, but same parents), John W., Mary, Amos L., and

Elender (possibly Eleanor or Ellen) Nov. 27, 1876 age 91y 7d.

"If you need dates on any of the others, let me know.

"Melinda."

At last I had found it! The final resting place of Sarah Eleanor Lee, described to me when I was a little boy by my now deceased great aunt Olive as an "aristocratic woman who did a lot of knitting and not much talking." I imagined her sitting in her quiet resting place in a weed filled cemetery by the side of a lonely highway, surrounded by winter corn fields in the middle of the vast desert expanse of Indiana. She was completely forgotten... until now!

Maybe Sarah Eleanor Lee went by the name of Eleanor Lee? I did a quick search on rootsweb.com and found an Eleanor Lee, granddaughter to Richard Henry Lee, and daughter of Thomas Lee, born in 1783. That was close to the year 1785 from her tombstone (based on how old she was when she died), but she was listed as having a different spouse and dying in Virginia. I felt like I was getting closer, but not quite.

I got another email from Melinda

"Doug,

"There are a lot of other people in this cemetery, too. Are they all related?

"Also...I have some Ruggels in my own family tree. In recent generations, I have a cousin, Jeffrey Eckstein, married to an Adrienne Ruggels (early 40s).

"In earlier generations:

"Descendants of Samuel Ruggles

"Generation No. 1

"1. SAMUEL1 RUGGLES He married ANNA BRIGHT.

"Child of SAMUEL RUGGLES and ANNA BRIGHT is:

"[and then she continued with the rest of her family tree]"

I wrote back:

"Melinda,

"You can go to www.bremnerhistory.com and click on Wilson, and that is the entire clan that was buried in that cemetery. I also attach a genealogy report of that family who were in Shelby Co., looks like Moral Township (is that a real place?). I am going to go through your information now. I don't recognize any of your current ancestors although with a strange name like Ruggels (Ruggles, Ruggals, etc.) they had to be related in a rural area like that.

"Doug"

She wrote back

"Doug,

"Moral Township is real (oddly enough). If you go to our web site (www.rootsweb.com/~inshelby/index.htm) you will find the township maps. You should be able to print one out for yourself.

"My Ruggels connections weren't here in Shelby County. The most recent generation is in Dubois County. The others were in New England. I will try to get to your web site to look at the names. I'm preparing for my finals for next week, so I'm not sure when I will be squeezing in time for extra stuff...

"Thanks,

"Melinda.

Jake Ehrlich III called me back. He sounded concerned about my voice mail.

"My grandfather was known to be somewhat of a philanderer," he said. "If someone calls and claims to be a long, lost relative, that makes me concerned. By the way, I looked up your sister's web site. Is she married?"

I didn't have a quick answer for the grandson of Jacob Ehrlich.

We exchanged more information, and came to the conclusion that, although our two Jacob Ehrlichs may have been distant cousins in the old country, they were not one and the same person.

Denise Ehrlich sent me several more death certificates, including one for Laura Anita Schemmel, the first wife of our common grandfather, Edward Joseph Ehrlich. She was born December 11, 1907, in Hillyard City (outside of Spokane), married Edward Joseph Ehrlich on August 10, 1926, in Hillyard, and had a son named Edward Joseph Ehrlich II, on November 14, 1927. She died of polio at the young age of 21, just one year after the birth of her son, on September 16, 1928, in Spokane.

The death certificate of Fred Rosenberg, Jr., arrived in the mail from the King County Vital Records Department. Sure enough, in addition to information about his birth and death, it listed the "informant" name as Howard Rosenberg (son), 1924 8th Ave W, Everett, WA, 98204. Using online search services, I was able to track a David Rosenberg, who previously lived in Everett, Washington, and now was living in Union, Washington, a small town on Hood Canal (which is not really a canal, just a part of Puget Sound). I looked up his number and gave him a call.

"Hello," a gruff voiced person said at the other end of the line.

"Howard Rosenberg?" I asked.

"Yes."

"I am doing some research on my family tree and I wanted to ask you a few questions. Are you related to a Fred Rosenberg who was born in Canada?"

"Who are you and how did you find out about me," he angrily fired back.

I felt stumped. Because I have been using online services to track your addresses for the past 30 years? Because I managed to track down, through sheer persistence, birth and death records on many of your family members?

"I am looking for information about a woman named Alice Rosenberg who married a man named Woods," I responded, desperate to keep him on the line.

"I am a Vietnam veteran with posttraumatic stress disorder," he said. "I don't remember what happened last week, let alone 30 years ago."

"But you don't remember an aunt named Alice Woods?" I insisted.

"I don't know anything about my family, ask my sister." And with that he gave me the number of his sister, Jeannie Rosenberg McEldowney, from Kingsport, Washington, a town on Puget Sound further north from Union.

I called Jeannie. "Yes, I remember Aunt Alice, "She was married to a man named Fred Gran. He was disabled, and she took care of him for many years. He was a veteran and died at the Seattle Veterans Administration Hospital."

"And was she ever married to a man named William Woods?"

"I'm not sure. I don't know a lot about her earlier life."

"Did she have any children?" I asked.

"She had a son who is still alive and living in Tacoma, Washington. I'll have to ask him if it is OK for you to contact him."

"What about a daughter named Myra J. Woods?"

"Not that I know of."

After I hung up the phone I pondered this mystery. How could Jeannie have had contact with Alice, know about her son but not her daughter? I still couldn't explain how Alice would have left her husband and one year old daughter, traveled by herself hundreds of miles to Spokane, Washington, and then gotten pregnant with another man and delivered a child, which she subsequently put up for adoption.

I pulled out the adoption papers again. The papers clearly stated that the Alice Woods, mother of my mother, was born in Washington State, and that this was her first child. Alice Rosenberg Woods Gran was born in Canada, and already had a child by 1932, the year of my mother's birth. Why would she lie about that? Or how could she forget that she had a child? That wasn't possible. Either she had to be lying, or this was the wrong Alice Woods. I wrote away to the King County (i.e. Seattle) Vital Records Department for a copy of Alice's death certificate.

I paid for a subscription to ancestry.com and started looking for an alternative Alice Pauline Woods. There was a Pauline Woods, born August 23, 1913, in Washington State. That would be the right place of birth, but the birth year was a little off. An Alice Woods, who died in Los Angeles, was born in Mississippi in 1913, but both the birth place and year of birth were off.

There was an Alice Woods in the 1920 U.S. Census living in Lefloe County, Mississippi. She was the daughter of Will Woods, and under "race or color" was listed as "B" for black. That would explain the 4% sub Saharan African in my DNA report. But she was six years old in 1920, making her birth year about 1914, a couple of years off of the Alice Woods listed on my mother's birth certificate. I also found an Alice Woods, also black, and born in 1912 in Roanoke, Virginia. I wrote away to the City of Roanoke but they were unable to find a birth certificate for her.

I emailed my family about the news of my DNA analysis.

"They always said your mother was a Black Norwegian," my father said.

"She may have been Black, but I don't know about the Norwegian," I replied.

"I don't know if you should trust those DNA tests," my father testily replied. "Besides there were waves of different people passing through Europe in the Middle Ages. It is possible that some of those genes mixed up with our ancestors."

"There were not waves of sub Saharan Africans passing through Europe, Dad," I said. "The only possible explanation is that one of our ancestors in the US mated with someone of African descent. The test said 4%, with a range of 2-6. And that range did not include 0, so there is not a possibility that there is no sub Saharan African blood in our line, unless there is something grossly wrong with the test itself."

"If we were living in Louisiana in the 19th Century, we'd be classified as coloreds, and have no rights," was my brother's comment.

Skimming through my bookshelf that weekend, I pulled out a book by William Faulkner called Light in August. I read the book straight through over the next couple of weeks. It was about a man named "Christmas" who lived in the South back in the 1930s. He looked white, but was illegitimate. His biological father was a light colored mulatto. The father of his mother cursed him. Eventually he was killed by an angry mob as a "nigger" because he had that drop of African blood in him. I thought, even though to look in the mirror you wouldn't know it, that well could be me. I must say that I felt a more personal connection with the plight of downtrodden African-Americans at that point than I ever had previously in my life.

I followed up on the background of Edward Joseph Ehrlich. I learned from ancestry.com that his brother, Harold ("Hal"), took the Conlon name of their step-father, Thomas Conlon, as his legal name. A search of the Social Security Death Index showed that he died in Spokane, on May 29, 1988. I emailed Charles Hansen of the Eastern Washington Genealogical Society and asked his volunteers to look up the obituaries on Hal Conlon and his wife Emma Powers Conlon (formerly Emma Powers Ehrlich), in the local paper, the Spokesman Review. I received copies of the obituaries several weeks later.

The Spokesman Review on February 11, 1952, had the following obituary for Tom Conlon:

"Thomas J. Conlon, 78, E2123 Central, Spokane resident for 50 years, died yesterday at a Spokane hospital. He had been hospitalized for three weeks.

"Rosary will be said at 8:30 tonight at Hennessey funeral home. A requiem mass will be celebrated at 9 am tomorrow at St. Patrick's church by the Rev. Victor Henderer, S.J. Burial will be in Holy Cross cemetery.

"A retired carpenter, Mr. Conlon helped construct Sacred Heart hospital and Mount St. Michael's scholasticate. He was born at Prescott, Ont., and was a member of St. Patrick's parish.

"Surviving are the widow, Emma K., at the home; a son, Harold J., Spokane; two daughters, Mrs. T.A. Beasley and Mrs. A.C. McDonald, both Spokane; a stepson, E.J. Ehrlich, in California, and nine grandchildren."

For Emma Powers Conlon, the October 8, 1962, Spokesman Review had the following obituary, entitled "Death Takes Mrs. Conlon at Age 80."

"Mrs. Emma K. Conlon, 80, formerly a resident at E2123 Central, died Sunday at a local hospital. She had lived in Spokane for 58 years.

"Mrs. Conlon was a member of Local 400, Hotel and Restaurant Employees' Union.

"She is survived by two sons, Hal. J. Conlon, Spokane, and Edward J. Conlon, Long Beach, Calif.: two daughters, Mrs. Ted Beasley and Mrs. Ileen McDonald, both Spokane; two brothers, Edward and Jack Powers, both of San Francisco, Calif.; two sisters, Mrs. Nellie O'Connor, San Francisco, and Sister Mary Greta, Bethany Convent, St. Paul, Minn.; 12 grandchildren and 14 great-grandchildren.

"The body is at Hennessey Funeral Home."

I looked up the U.S. Census for Spokane in 1910. Jacob and Emma Ehrlich were living with their children, Edward J. and Harold S., with Jacob's occupation listed as Mail Clerk for the Railway, and Emma as Landlady. His parents were listed as born in Germany, and her birth and her parents in Canada.

The 1920 U.S. Census for Spokane listed Thomas Conlon living with wife Anna K., and children Eileen, Annie, Edward and Hal. His occupation was listed as carpenter.

So what happened to Jacob Ehrlich? It appeared that Emma had re married and brought the boys with her to this new home.

I emailed Charles Hansen again and asked him to look up obituaries for Hal (Ehrlich) Conlon and Edward Joseph Ehrlich II, based on the date of deaths I got from his Social Security Index entry.

I went back to Laura Anita Schemmel, first wife of Edward Joseph Ehrlich. I looked up the 1930 U.S. Census on ancestry.com, and found a Daniel and Sophie Schemmel living in Spokane with Edward Joseph Ehrlich, age 2. Daniel worked as a machinist for the Railway. Those had to be the parents of Laura Schemmel. A copy of the Spokane 1910 Census showed Daniel and Sophie Schemmel living with their children Harry, age 14, and Laura, age 2. That confirmed that Daniel and Sophie Shemmel were the parents of Laura Schemmel.

I gave Denise Ehrlich a call.

"It looks like Edward Joseph Ehrlich shipped off his son Edward Joseph Jr. to live with his grandparents after his mother died."

"My grandfather never talked about him very much," she said. "He seemed to think that he was a bad person."

"He certainly didn't help him very much by dumping him after Laura died." I said. "And he must have hooked up with my mother's mother not long after Laura died, sometime in 1931 based on my mother's birth date in 1932. I saw that Emma Powers was in a Hotel Workers Union."

"She worked in the Davenport Hotel, and my grandfather worked there for a while busing tables."

If Edward Joseph Ehrlich was dating someone at the time that his young son was being raised by his in-laws, the Schemmels, wouldn't they know something about it? I decided to try and find out more information about them. I found Daniel Shemmels Washington State Death Certificate. It listed a date of death of January 24, 1965. I wrote away for his obituary.

A few weeks later I got the obituaries in the mail for Hal Conlon and Edward Joseph Ehrlich II, as well as the Schemmels, from Charles Hansen.

Hal Conlon's obituary read:

"Passed away May 29, 1988 in Spokane. Survived by his children, Dr. Tom Conlon, Liberty Lake, WA. Mrs. Darrell (Connie)

Frigaard, Spokane, and Jeff Conlon, Tacoma, WA; nine grandchildren..."

The Spokesman Review of January 26, 1965 had the following obituary for Daniel Schemmel.

"SCHEMMEL, Daniel A. (90) – His home, E2320 Diamond. A 60-year resident of Spokane. A member of St. Patrick's Parish. He was a retired machinist for Great Northern Railway. Survived by his wife, Laura, at the home; one son, Harry Schemmel, Spokane; 3 grandchildren; 4 great-grandchildren; one half-sister, Mrs. Amelia Thompson, Wapakoneta, Ohio. Rosary Wed., Jan 27, at 8:30 pm in the IRIS CHAPEL of the HENNESSEY FUNERAL HOME, N2203 DIVISION ST. Funeral service Thurs., Jan. 28, at 9:30 am from St. Patrick's Church, Queen & Nelson. The Very Rev. Robert C. O'Neil officiating. Interment Riverside Memorial Park."

In the earlier census records his wife had been listed as Sophia. If his surviving wife was Laura Schemmel that meant that he had remarried. I searched for a Laura Schemmel in the Washington State Death Certificates, and found one who died on May 8, 1971, in Spokane. I requested a lookup of her obituary.

I then jumped on the internet and started looking for a Dr. Tom Conlon, listed in Hal Conlon's obituary as his son. Drs. were always an easy hit since they frequently show up in various listings and public documents. I found a Dry Tom Conlon practicing dentistry in the Spokane area and gave him a call.

"This is Dr. Bremner calling Dr. Conlon," I said to the receptionist.

"Is this in regards to a patient?" she replied.

"Not exactly," I replied. "I'll have to fill in the doctor with more of the details when I talk to him."

Later that afternoon I got a call back from Dr. Tom Conlon.

"This isn't exactly a clinically related call," I said. "I think I am the grandson of Edward Joseph Ehrlich, the brother of your father, Harold (Hal) Conlon."

After some discussion we determined that this was probably the case.

"My father wrote a book called Roots, which was a history of the family. It must be in my garage somewhere, but I am not sure where it is. I don't know much about our family history. You should talk to my sister, Connie."

And then he gave me the number of his sister, Connie Conlon Martin, who was currently married to Lannie Martin, and previously married to Darrell Frigaard.

"I remember the book Roots," Connie said on the phone. "I don't know where it is. We really don't have any other records beyond that. But if you want to come out to Spokane you are always welcome."

Connie told me more about Emma Powers and her children. After Jacob Ehrlich abandoned his family in the first part of the 20th Century, Emma Powers was not able to support herself and her two small boys in Spokane. She went back to her native Canada, and she parked her boys in French speaking orphanages in the provinces of either Quebec or Ontario. She probably met her second husband, Thomas Conlon, there, who was born in Prescott, Ontario, Canada, a town on the US border. He probably helped her get the boys out of the orphanage and return to Spokane. Harold (Hal) legally adopted the name of Conlon; Edward used the name of Conlon only once, when he falsely reported it as his last name as father of Baby Jane Doe, daughter of Alice, in Spokane Washington in 1932. His legal name was Edward Joseph Ehrlich. She told me that he had a first wife who died young. They had a child, Edward Joseph Ehrlich II, who was a troublemaker and got arrested for armed robbery, for which he spent time in San Quentin prison. She didn't know what had happened to him.

I got the obituary of Laura Schemmel, second wife of Daniel Schemmel. Maybe tracking down the Schemmels would provide a clue about who Alice was. The obituary listed surviving children, one of whom was Mrs. Arthur Hoffman of Deer Park, Washington (Just north of Spokane). I logged onto whitepages.com and quickly found Arthur Hoffman (and his wife Sadie Maxfield Hoffman).

"My wife's mother was named Laura Agnes Loftin, she was the second wife of Daniel Schemmel," Arthur Hoffman told me. "She had four children from a previous marriage to Arther Maxfield, one of whom is my wife Sadie."

"Did you ever know an Edward Joseph Ehrlich, Daniel Schemmel's grandson?" I asked.

"Yes, they raised him from the time he was a small child. His mother had died and his father didn't want to take care of him. He was a very difficult child, very rebellious, and always getting in trouble. After a certain point they couldn't deal with him, and he left. He got into trouble with the law after that, but later he came back to Deer Park and owned a service station. He died here a few years back."

I thanked him and went back to my internet search. I found out that Edward Joseph Ehrlich Jr died in Deer Park on February 28, 1998. I wrote away to request an obituary lookup.

In February of 2006, the death certificate of Alice Rosenberg arrived in the mail from the King County Vital Records office. It listed her maiden name as "Alice Gertrude Rosenberg", not consistent with the "Alice Pauline Woods" on my mother's birth certificate. I remembered that she was born in Canada, not in Washington, as stated on my mother's birth certificate. This also would have been her second child, not her, as stated on my mother's birth certificate.

Was Alice Rosenberg my grandmother? Did I have the wrong Alice Rosenberg, or was I on the wrong trail altogether?

Chapter 9

According to the traditions and tenants of the LDS Church, following the "ordinances of the temple," a volunteer is baptized as a substitute for the dead person who never had the chance to be baptized during their time here on Earth. Once they go to heaven, the Mormons believe, these people are given a choice as to whether they become part of the church. But if they aren't identified, they won't have the choice. And if they aren't identified, they have only their descendants who have converted to Mormonism to blame. Thus, for the true believers of the Mormon faith, genealogy is literally religion.

As of 1991, 113 million people were introduced posthumously to the LDS church.

The Mormon Church slowly grew from 30,000 members in 1840 to one million in 1950 (mostly in Utah) to over 10 million in 1999 and 14.1 million in 2010. The highest concentration of Mormons are in the tiny South Pacific Ocean nation of Tonga, with 40% of the population converted. As a scientist looking at the growth curve of the LDS church, my conclusion is that they have exponential growth. And most of the growth is outside the US.

Why is a religion that states that Jesus came to Utah so appealing to people from Tonga? Does their emphasis on being promoted to heaven as a family unit have anything to do with it? Is this eternal bliss, or the family reunion from hell?

Curious, I looked up the LDS website. It had a series of faces with questions under them.

One of them was a serene looking African-American man. "What is family?" said the caption.

What, indeed?

Had the Mormons really fallen onto something? That connecting with the nodes of your family, those linked to you by sperm and eggs and DNA, looping simultaneously backward and forward through space and time, like the drooping lines connecting the electricity towers that move through mowed swaths of forest in the rural parts of America, will lead you to paradise? Based on my current obsession and internet addiction for searching genealogy on the web, I was in no condition to say no.

With the onset of the internet and computer technology, the Mormons have a powerful tool to identify their ancestors. In a practice common to many genealogists, they attempt to identify everyone related to them, both directly and indirectly, in the idea that the indirect ancestors may lead to clues about unidentified ancestors more directly in their family line. The Mormons don't think that the internet and computers are an accident. They think it is sacred technology, part of God's plan to give them the tools to identify all of their ancestors, and lead them toward the exalted station in the afterlife they all strive for.

Ancestry.com is a private company based in Utah that was founded by members of the Mormon church. Ancestry is like MTV to a growing section of Americans, baby boomers, most of whom are not Mormons, who are getting the religion of genealogy (if not the religion of Joseph Smith's tablets).

Chapter 10

The more I thought about the Alice Rosenberg I had identified in my research, the more unlikely it seemed that she was my grandmother. Not only did the family not feel like the right fit. Granted that the name Alice Pauline Woods was probably made up, but my intuition told me that she would not lie about her middle name in addition to her last name. And Alice Rosenberg's middle name was Gertrude, not Pauline. Alice's place of birth in Canada did not match the Washington place of birth of the mother on the birth certificate, and the birth order of children (second, not first), were also not right. My gut told me she would lie about her last name, to avoid shame and protect her family from disgrace. But she would not lie about everything. It also seemed unlikely for her to move from Seattle to Spokane, and then back to Seattle again, where she married another man.

I still had not solved the mystery of who William Woods and Myra J. Woods were, but I figured that was a mystery best solved by those who would be most interested in the mystery, the people who were actually related to Alice Rosenberg Woods Gran. I packed up all of the birth and death certificates and other information related to my research on the Rosenbergs, and mailed them off to Jeannie Rosenberg McEldowney of Kingston, Washington.

Then who was the real Alice Woods? In my experience from the research I had done so far, it wasn't often that someone simply vanished from the vast database of the United States. If they have ever held a job, had a social security number, died, married, gone into debt, been born or baptized, had children, went to jail, or had any interaction with their communities that warranted minimal interest, they become well documented in the world wide web, in addition to the vast archives of ancestry.com and other online services that are being utilized by a growing legion of genealogy fanatics.

I got back onto the Rosenberg trail. I emailed a "lookup" volunteer I found on the internet to check obituaries in Coeur D'Alene Idaho. After a few weeks I got back the following reply,

"FRED A ROSENBERG, 78

"Fred A. Rosenberg, 78, Coeur d' Alene, Rte. 2, Box 161, a resident here since 1958, died Sunday at his home after a sudden illness.

"He was born in Vancouver, Canada, in 1892.

"Mr. Rosenberg, and his wife, Dollie A. Rosenberg, came to Coeur d' Alene from Seattle after his retirement.

"He was employed as an electrician for Continental Can Co., Seattle.

"He attended the Episcopal Church.

"Survivors include his wife, at the home; a son, Fred P. Rosenberg, a daughter, Mrs. Alice Gran, both of Seattle; three grandchildren, six great-grandchildren, and a sister in Canada.

"Funeral services are pending at the English Funeral Chapel.

"Coeur d' Alene Press, Monday, December 7, 1970."

The Social Security Death Index said that Flora Hurn Rosenberg had died in Seattle in 1954, so Fred must have remarried after her death.

I got the obituary for Edward Joseph Ehrlich Jr in the mail. It listed surviving children as Mrs. Barbara Kosiorek, Mrs. Laura Connley, and Edward Joseph Ehrlich III. One of the grandchildren listed was Sarah Carver. I looked up the names on whitepages.com and mailed them letters asking if we might be related. I felt like I was getting a little far afield and didn't know if these people wanted to be contacted, but my inability to get leads on Alice was making me desperate.

A week later I got a call.

"My name is Sarah Carver from Spokane, and I got your letter," she said.

"I sent out letters to several people hoping that one of them might match."

"We all got the letters," she said.

"So you are related to Edward Joseph Ehrlich II?" I asked.

"My mother was Fern Bates. Edward was not my biological father. He was my step-father. My own father was pretty shaky. I spent much of my early childhood living out of our car. When my mother married Edward, it was actually a stabilizing influence in my life."

"And is there an Edward Joseph Ehrlich III?"

"He's my half-brother."

"Where does he live?"

"Idaho," she answered vaguely, with a touch of suspicion.

I was starting to wonder if I wanted to be prying into these people's lives. Edward Joseph Ehrlich III could be in jail himself for all I knew.

"I understand Edward Joseph Ehrlich II had some legal problems."

"Yeah, we didn't find out till later. When my mother found out he was in jail, she said she would never have married an ex-convict. Why did you contact us anyway?"

"I'm doing some research on my family tree. I wanted to ask some questions, like the names of your brothers and sisters, and when they were born."

"What do you want to know that for?" she asked suspiciously.

I was starting to wonder if this was such a good idea. I didn't know anything about these people.

"I'm trying to fill out my family tree. It's like a hobby," I said.

My wife was calling me to come downstairs to lunch.

"OK, I guess," she said.

"How about if I call you back," I said.

"No, I can help you with your family tree. That's OK."

"I have your address. I'll just send you a list of questions." I said good-bye and hung up.

Chapter 11

In *Finding Our Fathers: A Guide to Jewish Genealogy*, author Dan Rottenberg wrote, "Jews have not traditionally been interested in genealogy. For most of our history a coat of arms was something that you ran from." However the Jews have been better than any other group at maintaining their ethnic identity and remembering where they came from.

I was scheduled to travel to New York City for a scientific conference in the Spring of 2006. Before I left I looked up some places to go and do Jewish genealogy research in New York. I knew that Joseph Ehrlich had lived briefly in 1880 at 401 East 65 Street in New York, based on his naturalization papers, which listed his occupation as "Gardiner".

It was a sunny but pleasantly cool Spring morning when I walked down 65th Street in Manhattan, hunting for the address of my ancestor's former resident. It was pretty obvious that the high rise luxury apartment building located at 401 East 65th Street didn't exist in 1880. I tried to picture in my mind's eye what it must have looked like in 1880, without much luck.

I hopped on a subway and went downtown to the Jewish History Center in New York, hoping to do some research.

When I entered the building, a man in traditional Jewish religious dress sat at the counter.

"May I help you?" he said.

I couldn't feel more out of place.

"I want to do some family research," I said.

He motioned upstairs.

I followed a sign toward the research library. There was a handful of other people peering at computer screens and sitting at a series of tables looking through books and other documents. I looked at some of the materials on the shelves and fished around on one of the computers. I didn't find anything useful. Obviously the people at the Jewish Center weren't going to give me the key to the lost history of my Jewish ancestors.

As I sat there surrounded by other genealogy researchers, I thought about my ancestors, Edward Joseph Ehrlich, and his deceased wife Laura Schemmel. Even the Rosenbergs, whose dreams of a better life made them keep moving with every generation. I started to wonder if I was making them come alive in some way, if not in the afterlife, at least in some type of ethereal world, which is the shared knowledge on one's ancestors.

I had learned by searching ship lists on ancestry.com, that Joseph Ehrlich was a Jew who immigrated to this country from what was then Bohemia, or part of Austria or Germany, and currently is the Czech Republic. Like so many others, he travelled to this country on a ship with his wife and infant son, Jacob. As a Jew, he and his family had maintained a strong sense of where they came from for 2,000 years.

On July 12, 1879, Joseph Ehrlich and his family arrived in New York on board the *Maine*, which had set sail from Bremen, Germany, a few months before. He was naturalized in New York, moved to Cleveland, and later Spokane, where he worked as a meat cutter. Within the next 30 years, his son Jacob would walk away from his family, and his grandson Edward Joseph would deny he was a Jew, and become baptized Catholic.

In 1870 Bohemia, the Jews were required to live in villages set aside just for them. They had severe restrictions on their travel, and by law were only allowed to have one son, ostensibly to limit the growth of the Jewish population. Whether by explicit requirement of due to their own customs and religion, they were easily identified as Jews by their style of clothing, the way they wore their hair, and their behavior. They knew exactly who they were and where they came from, and that hadn't changed in over a thousand years.

And yet, in the course of a few generations, the Ehrlichs had forgotten all of that. They didn't know where they came from. They forgot that they were once Jews. They thought they had always been Catholics. They wandered around the country and forgot who their family was.

I had started out to find out who my mother was, but found out much more along the way.

Chapter 12

When I got back from New York, I returned to the task of finding Alice, the mother of my mother. I started to consider the possibility that some of the information on the birth of my mother was incorrect. This would mean that she had violated the law, since she took a sworn oath when she signed the adoption papers. I wondered, if my grandmother lied under oath, was my mother's adoption legal?

I once again pulled out my files. The adoption records said that the mother was 'Alice Pauline Woods' and the father was "Edward Conlon". The record gave an address for Edward Conlon, and listed the address of Alice Woods as being with Edith Gilbert in Spokane. The legal papers from the adoption listed Edith Gilbert as the legal custodian of the child. There were legal papers where the mother had signed over the child to Edith Gilbert as the legal guardian.

I had copies of materials that my sister had sent me a few years ago that I had never looked at carefully before. She received them from my mother's adoptive sister, Vinnie Cooper. Originally they were the property of my mother's adoptive, Madeline Cooper.

There was a baby book where Madeline Cooper recorded various details of my mother's birth and early developmental milestones. There were also numerous letters from Mrs. Gilbert to the adoptive parents. The mother of my mother was pregnant out of wedlock, and by the necessity of the times had to live with a "birthing mother" (in this case Mrs. Gilbert) until the baby was born, so that the public presence of her pregnant state would not cause a scandal. At the end of this period it was expected that she would put the baby up for adoption, and that would be the end of the embarrassing scene.

My best guess was that my grandmother gave false testimony under oath about her name, saying she was Alice Pauline Woods, when it was something else. That made the legal proceedings of my mother's adoption invalid under the law.

I also found a typed letter from 1930 from Lyndle Cooper to the Eastern Washington Children's Home. He was requesting an application to adopt a child. I did some research on the internet and found out that the home no longer existed, but the records were kept by an organization in Seattle. I called them up.

"We have no record of a Lyndle Cooper adopting a child from the home," said a kind voice at the other end of the line. "Are you looking for a person related to you?"

"Yes, I'm looking for my mother," I said. "She died when I was four years old. She was adopted, and I only had the adoption records opened 10 years ago. I'm not sure if any of her biological family is still alive, or if they even want to hear from me."

"I went through the same process myself," she said. "Nine times out of ten both sides are happy that they connected with each other again."

"But I don't understand why there is no record of my mother coming from the home," I said. "My mother had to have come from somewhere."

"Not all children came from adoption agencies or children's homes. At that time all you needed was a doctor to sign the paperwork for you."

After I hung up the phone I thought some more. I assumed that my mother came through an adoption agency. But if what the woman at the children's home said was true? What if Dr. Hall had made arrangements with Edith Gilbert and the Coopers, as well as the biological mother, to have my mother put up for adoption with no involvement from an adoption agency or anyone else? If so, that meant that there was some kind of connection between the Coopers and my grandmother.

I decided to look at this mysterious Edith Gilbert more carefully. Why did she let a 19-year-old woman live with her in secrecy until she gave birth to an illegitimate and unwanted baby, who would be later given up for adoption? Was she just doing it for the money? Did she have any ulterior motives? Did she have any connection with the family?

I looked up Edith Gilbert's date of death on ancestry.com. I next wrote away for a lookup service to send me the obituary of Edith Gilbert from the Spokane newspaper. I got the following.

"Edith Cleo Gilbert

"Private family service was held for Edith Cleo (Scamahorn) Gilbert, former longtime Spokane resident, who died Wednesday in Dallas, Oregon. She was 97.

"Burial is to be at Riverside Memorial Park in Spokane with the Dallas Mortuary Chapel in charge of arrangements.

"Born in Illinois, she came to Cheney in 1903 and married Edwin Gilbert in 1913. He died in 1919.

"Mrs. Gilbert worked in aircraft production as a riveter during World War II. She also worked for the Shriners Hospital for Crippled Children as an attendant for 10 years.

"She was a member of Queen Avenue United Methodist Church in Spokane.

"Mrs. Gilbert moved in 1975 from Spokane to Dallas.

"Survivors include one son, Roger Gilbert of Dallas, one daughter, Letha Bergstrom of Dallas, four grandchildren, 10 great grandchildren, and eight great-great-grandchildren.

"Service is scheduled for 10 a.m. Pontchard Chapel at Fort Cemetery. A memorial service to follow Wednesday in Dallas, Oregon."

I thought that it was strange that Edith Gilbert would end up in the small town of Dallas, Oregon, the same town that Madeline Cooney Cooper was born in. Was this more than a coincidence?

Edith's husband was listed in her obituary as Edwin Gilbert. I looked up census data for 1920 and 1930, and found them in Cheney, Washington, a wheat farming town south of Spokane, with occupation listed as "farmer". I was able to determine through the census that Edwin had a brother named Frank Gilbert. After Edwin died, Edith moved to Spokane. Her brother-in-law, Frank Gilbert, continued to be a wheat farmer in Cheney, Washington. By a strange coincidence, the father of my mother's

118

mother was also a wheat farmer in Cheney at that time. In addition, Lyndle Cooper, my mother's adoptive father, also was a resident. Since the census goes house to house, people on the same page are neighbors. When I looked up the census, I could see that they were actually neighbors.

Frank must have known both the family of the biological mother and the Coopers. Learning of the inconvenient pregnancy, and knowing of the Cooper's desire to have a child, he suggested using his widowed sister in Spokane as a birthing mother. The group arranged with Dr. Hall to sign the paperwork. I even found out that Edith had family with the last name of Woods, suggesting how they arrived at the fictitious last name for Alice.

I pulled out my mother's baby book again. I read the list of people who had signed the baby book as having coming to visit my mother soon after she was born. At the top of the page was written "Mr. and Mrs. Frank Gilbert." Now that was more than coincidence. It became immediately and painfully clear to me at that point that the people who had "adopted" my mother not only knew who she was in advance, but knew everything about her biological parents, and in fact knew her biological family personally.

I called some of the people on the baby book to try and get some more answers. I talked to an octogenarian who knew the wheat farmers listed on the baby book, but didn't have a lot of new information to give me. When I gave her an overview of what I was trying to do, she gave me her opinion that young people shouldn't have sexual relations outside of marriage.

How interesting, I thought. But that still didn't tell me who Alice was.

Sitting in my home library overlooking Ponce de Leon Ave, a busy thoroughfare in Atlanta, Georgia, I thought about all of the pieces to the puzzle that I had assembled so far. The adoption was clearly arranged between parties that knew each other. This information seemed oddly familiar. Based on what?

As a scientist, I knew that it was always good to keep stray pieces of information and facts that don't fit into a story in the back of your mind, and not discard them. That way, if new information comes along, it might come in handy in solving the puzzle. I thought about the family lore and things I had been told in the past.

My father once said that he thought that my mother's adoptive parents knew the biological parents. He tried to get the information out of 'Grandma Cooper', but she refused to tell anyone until she died.

I remembered my sister, Lynn, wrote a letter along with copies of some family pictures after my mother's adoptive sister, Vinnie Cooper, had gone to meet her for the first time a few years ago. I had never met Vinnie, at least at any time since my early childhood. We lost contact with my mother's adoptive family after her death. Vinnie's search for our family and her visit to my sister occurred after the death of her own mother, Madeline Cooney Cooper, and seemed to have been stimulated by what she learned before her mother died.

I pulled out the letter from my sister. "Vinnie said that she knew the half-sister of our mother, and that she was in the same class with her at Reardan Elementary School. Her name was Elinore Flood." Was that the secret the dying Madeline Cooney Cooper told to Vinnie back in 1992 that caused Vinnie to go see my sister? I pulled out my map. I found Reardan, a small town about 30 miles west of Spokane, in the middle of wheat farming country.

I called my sister. She confirmed what was in the letter, and said she would call Vinnie. I got impatient and looked up Vinnie in whitepages.com and gave her a call myself, even though I had not spoken to her in any time that I could remember.

"Elinore Flood was in my class at Reardan Elementary," she said. "She was very smart and skipped a grade, so that she ended up in my class. She was a little uppity though, and I thought she felt like she was better than everyone else. Her mother was a teacher at Reardan Elementary, as was my mother."

"Did my mother know who she was?" I asked.

"She never did, although I always had an idea who Elinore was. My mother, Grandma Cooney, asked your mother if she wanted to learn more about her biological family. Your mother said that she already had a family, and didn't need anything more."

After I hung up the phone, I thought about it some more. My mother's biological mother taught school in a small town where her own daughter, who didn't know her, went to school.

My research showed that, given the connections between the two families, it was likely the mother knew who her daughter was, although she never publicly acknowledged her. How bizarre.

And why didn't my mother try to figure the situation out? Everything I heard about my mother was that she was a highly intelligent, intellectual, and curious person. With all of those qualities, why shouldn't she be interested in where she came from, her roots and background? I certainly would be, and I couldn't imagine that she would be so much different.

I called up my father.

"I've been doing some research on Laurnell's family," I said. "I talked to Vinnie Cooper, and she said that Laurnell never wanted to know about her own biological family."

"That's nonsense," my father said. "I was constantly trying to get information out of Grandma Cooper, and she always refused. She said the truth was too terrible for us to know about."

That meant that Grandma Cooper knew who the parents of Laurnell were. It fit with the whole Elinor Flood story.

If that was the case, what did she think was too terrible for us to know? That she was Jewish? That she was part Black? That she was born out of wedlock?

I reflected on the sadness of the situation. So much effort to maintain appearances. Such tragic outcomes based on single decisions. The reverberation of psychological trauma through multiple families and multiple generations.

At that point, I had a number of clues, but no solid information. If Elinore Flood really was my mother's half sister, her last name was likely the name of her father, who would probably not have been the father of my mother, since she was listed on her adoption papers as born out of wedlock with the father of Edward Conlon (later identified as actually Edward Ehrlich).

I went back to the adoption papers. If Alice lied about some of the information on the birth certificate and adoption papers, as I felt was probable at that point, what would she be most likely to lie about?

I already established that the father, Edward Ehrlich (a.k.a. Conlon), told some little white lies about his true last name, but had provided an accurate address. If Alice lied, would she lie about everything?

I guessed that the answer was no. After all, she was taking a legal oath that what she was saying was true. She probably would have been motivated to minimize the number of lies she told, even though that wouldn't protect her from contempt of court if she were caught and someone wanted to pursue the issue. So what would she choose to lie about?

Most likely she would lie about her last name. She may have thought that this would be enough to make her untraceable. After all, she either felt she was protecting her family, and/or was coerced into giving up the child for adoption, for the motivation of avoiding scandal and shame, since it looked like the family had enough money to help her raise the child. To do that, she would have to falsify her last name.

Other than that, there was no motivation to lie about anything else. That meant that there was a good chance that the other information in the adoption papers, including her first and middle name, her state of birth, her age, and the number of previous children, were accurate.

That meant that I was looking for an Alice Pauline _____, age 19, born in Washington State, with no prior children, who had a child born out of wedlock in 1932.

That much I felt confident was true.

Furthermore, if what Vinnie Cooper said was true, she had a daughter named Elinore Flood, who was only a couple of years younger than my mother. If she had married, which was likely, both she and her second daughter would have a different last name.

Would that name be Alice Pauline Flood?

A search of obituaries in Spokane turned up an Alice Flood, mentioned in the obituary of a Lloyd Flood, who died January 15, 1999, in Spokane, Wash. His obituary in the *Spokane Spokesman Review* read:

"Funeral for Lloyd P. Flood, 86, was held Tuesday at Ball and Dodd Funeral Home-North. Entombment was at Fairmount Memorial Park.

"A longtime Spokane-area resident, Mr. Flood died Jan. 15.

"Born in Deep Creek, he graduated from Reardan (Wash.) High School and attended Gonzaga University before becoming a grain and cattle farmer in West Spokane County for many years.

"Mr. Flood and his wife of 57 years, Alice, lived in Chewelah, Wash., for several years before moving to Spokane in 1985.

"He was a lifetime member of the West Deep Creek Grange.

"His wife died in 1990.

"Survivors include a daughter, Elinor Iverson of Spokane; a brother, Seymour Flood of Reardan; a sister, Delores Fell of Westminster, Colo.; and two grandsons and two great-grandchildren.

"Memorial contributions may be made to the Hospice of Spokane, the American Cancer Society or the Lilac Blind Association."

That answered one of my big questions. If Alice Flood was my grandmother, she was no longer alive. However, Elinore Flood (now Elinore Iverson, undoubtedly because of a marriage to someone named Iverson), might still be alive.

I looked up an Elinor Iverson in whitepages.com in Spokane. I found a match. As I dialed the number my palms were sweating. There was an answering machine. I left my name and number.

"I am doing some research on my family and want to see if we are related," I said to the answering machine. It wasn't the first time I ever left a message like that.

Later that evening I got a return call.

"This is Elinor Iverson," said the voice on the other end of the line.

"I'm doing some research on my family and I want to see if we might be related," I said.

"How do you think we might be related?"

"Was your father named Lloyd Flood?"

"Yes he was."

"And was your mother named Alice Pauline?"

"Yes."

"Did she have any other children other than yourself?"

There was a pause at the other end of the line. "Why are you asking that?"

"I've been doing some research on my family, and I have reason to believe that your mother had a child out of wedlock before you were born, and before she married Lloyd Flood."

Silence. And then she spoke,

"I think your research may be correct. But I am going out to dinner tonight with my son," she said. "All of this is rather sudden. I am going to have to call you back later. I will call you back tomorrow."

As I hung up the phone, I felt a quickening of anticipation. This was the first possible connection to my mother, the first potential big payoff of my research, of my quest to find out who I was and where I came from.

I eagerly awaited the return phone call.

The next day she called me back on my cell phone.

"I think your research is correct," she said. "When I was young, I got a copy of my birth certificate. It said that I was the second child of my mother. I went to my father and asked him what did this mean? He got very angry and said never to talk about it again, that it would make my mother very upset. Many years later my Aunt Betty, just before she died, said that my mother had had another child before me and had given it up for adoption."

Joseph Ehrlich
1853-1951 Bohemia-Spokane — Jacob Ernest Ehrlish
Julia Kahn   b. 1878 Bohemia (Czech Rep.)
1855-1919 Bohemia-Spokane   d. ?   Edward Joseph Ehrlich
John Power   b. 1905 Spokane, Wash.
b ~1845 PEI Canada — Catherine Emma Powers   d. 1981 Los Angdeles, CA
Mary McNally   b. 1881 PEI, Canada
b. ~1860 PEI, Canada d. 1962 Spokane, WA   Madeline Laurnell Cooper

                     Henry Robert Lloyd
                     b. 1879 Wales
                     d. ~1955 Seattle, Wash.   Alice Pauline Lloyd
Ole Fjellingsdal   b. 1912 Spokane, Wash.
Norway   — Karen Fjellingsdal   d. 1990 Spokane, Wash.
Anna Solhiem   b. 1878 Norway
Norway   d. 1970 Seattle, Wash.

"So who were the parents of Alice?"

"Henry Lloyd was an emigrant from Wales. He married Karen Fjelingsdahl who emigrated from Norway. They were farmers in the Spokane area.

I had finally filled in the "other half" of my family tree. You can see the fruits of my labor here:

http://www.bremnerhistory.com/fig2.jpg

"Alice and her sisters, Betty and Anne, were school teachers. Alice loved to teach. They had a rule back then that you couldn't have kids if you were a female teacher. So while she was teaching at Reardan Elementary they sent me back to live with my grandparents in Four Lakes so they wouldn't know she had a child."

"Do you mind if I call you again?" I said.

"No, not at all." Later she sent me pictures.

Alice
graduation from
HS or EW

After I hung up the phone I checked my email. I had the following from Denise Ehrlich:

"I received this over the weekend and just now had a chance to scan it." [the death certificate of Laura Schemmel was attached]

"Good job!" I replied. "Maybe Edward was traumatized by the sudden death of Laura Schemmel and turned to Alice Woods for comfort. Is this starting to sound like a soap opera?

"Speaking of Alice Woods... I found her! My mother's birth certificate said her mother was

Alice Pauline Woods. I got the birth certificate of Alice Woods (Gran-Rosenberg), and her middle name was Gertrude. I talked to my mother's adoptive sister, who said my mother's half-sister was named Eleanor Flood. I searched on whitepages.com and couldn't find her. I looked for an Alice P. Flood in Spokane with the right birth year born in WA, and found her in an obituary for a Lloyd Flood, listed as the deceased wife. The obituary also listed his daughter, as Elinore Iverson (because of the strange name spelling I didn't make the connection at first). I found her right away on whitepages.com in Spokane and called her. She was pretty blown away. She actually went to grade school in a small town near Reardan with my mother.

"My mother's family knew she was her sister, but she had no idea. Elinore saw her birth certificate, which stated that she was the second born, but her father told her not to talk about it with her mother. Alice Pauline Lloyd was born in Four Lakes (which backs up the conspiracy theory about the baby 'adoption'). My mother was born in 1932 and Elinore in 1934. Elinore also had children, so I have many more relatives! I talked to her again today and she seemed to be getting pretty emotional about the whole thing and said it was traumatic to happen at age 72, but I told her it is never too late for the truth!

"On the Ehrlich side, as part of my general mania to come to closure I mailed letters to all of the possible addresses of the children of Ed E. III, who seem to have vanished from the face of the earth. I did find a Jewel Kosiorek, who could be a granddaughter, on the internet. She had a picture for her Christian Ministery group, in

Lubbock, Texas, and it looks like she went to Croatia on a mission."

Denise replied,

"Hi Doug,

"Wow! I'm glad you finally found the right Alice— did Elinore know what happened to the first husband, Mr. Woods? Remember, the census from 1930 that showed Alice married to M.E. Woods? They had been married approximately two years and had a two-month-old daughter named Myra J. Woods, Alice's parents and her brother Fred Rosenberg were living with them. I wonder what happened to Myra? So, I guess the Rosenberg descendants you spoke with are not the right ones?

"Such good stuff! I think the soap opera-esque aspect of this is what causes our mania for wanting to know the whole story. Our trees are getting pretty big. I'm thinking we/I should make a trip to Washington to meet some of our relatives. Maybe later we can plan a big reunion/meet our extended families. The stories would certainly be colorful.

"Cheers!

"Denise Ehrlich"

I replied,

"The Woods name was a total fabrication that Alice Pauline Lloyd invented to throw people off track in case they ever got a copy of the real certificate. I started to wonder when the Seattle Alice listed a middle initial of G. and that was confirmed when I got her death certificate with the name Alice Gertrude Rosenberg, so she is ruled out.

"The one I talked to the most, Jeannie (Rosenberg) McEldowney, said that Myra died young, sounded like in her 20s, and said Alice Rosenberg Woods Gran had another child named Jack. The death of Myra sounded mysterious. Jeannie seems to have no idea where she came from. I got the marriage certificate of W.E. Woods (William) and Alice . They have a lot of unspoken things in their family as well. I am going to give them a complete family history and mail all the birth certificates, etc., I got on them, but it is funny, it is difficult giving them up, even though they are not my family.

"I think a trip to Spokane would be good, if I could get my Italian wife to agree. Connie and Tom Conlon are really nice. Elinore said that Vinnie (my mother's adoptive sister) tried to arrange a meeting in Reardan where they all went to school together ten years ago, but Elinore didn't follow through. Elinore seems negative hearing about Edward Erhlich, who hit up her mother at an early age. A lot of people on that side of the family were teachers, and Elinore said you couldn't be married if you were a teacher, and that she was shipped off to (guess where!) Four Lakes for the first six years of her life to live with her grandparents, so her mother's school wouldn't figure out her mother was married. Bizarre?

"We used to have large family reunions on my father's side in Lynden (Whatcom Co) WA on 'grandpas farm' with about 100 people which were always a kick. Maybe we should set one up and let those who want to come, come. We are going to Europe this year but maybe could set up Summer of 2007.

"They must be looking down at us from Heaven saying, Damn it, they figured it out!

"Doug"

Denise replied,

"Okay, I think I've confused myself now. I understand the Alice Rosenberg Wood is no longer the right Alice. What was Alice Lloyd's maiden name and was she teaching when she conceived Laurnell? I'm still trying to figure out where the rest of your Jewish DNA came from on your mother's side.

"I guess I understand Elinore being disturbed about Edward Ehrlich and her mother. She is, after all, of that generation that would have tried to cover everything up and been deeply ashamed by it all. I hope she can get past that feeling since none of us are really concerned about past sins— well, except in so far as it reads like a soap opera and we are kind of addicted to it. We are just trying to figure out where we came from and who our extended family is. Did Elinore or Vinnie know Ed & Joe Ehrlich or the Conlons when they were growing up? I still don't have a good feel for the geography in the area, so I'm not sure how close together they all lived.

"So Elinore and Vinnie have been in touch all this time, but Elinore did not know she was Laurnell's half sister until you called her? Wow.....

"Cheers!

"Denise Ehrlich.

I replied,

"Thanks for the corrections, I updated my file.

"Another thing— what's with all the name funny business? Alice Woods is really Alice Lloyd, Edward Conlon is Edward Ehrlich...

"Fern Bates had two real husbands (Felch and Ehrlich), and I guess Carver, although I am not totally sure he was a husband, too, but he is the biological father of Sarah. I think things were pretty crazy for them, although now it sounds like things have quieted down. I assume the Edward Joseph Ehrlich III was the real McCoy, based on his name. He married Fern about 1966, per her story. The other thing I got was Mike Conley is husband of Laura (Federal Way) and Kaz Kosiorek (Deer Park) is the husband of Barbara (who died in 1994), and his daughter's name is Jewel. I think she said EJE III ('Joe') is in Montana. Ernest Felch was her other husband, and Ernest E. Felch, Jr., is in Arizona (listed Glendale on the obituary), but they don't keep up with him. Sarah is divorced with kids. She was called Ehrlich as a child and changed her name to her husband's name, but later changed her name legally to Carver (her Dad's name) after her divorce. Another name game! She has grown kids.

"I guess she is not our 'half cousin' biologically, but EJE III probably is and maybe Laura (???)

"I got the feeling that the kids had all already communicated with each other about the letters I sent."

"Hi Doug," she replied.

"The name thing certainly is complicated. I'm guessing Alice intentionally used the Conlon name on the adoption and birth certificate documents to throw everyone off— with or without Ed's knowledge. I wonder if Edward knew about Alice 's pregnancy? He probably did. He never went by the name Conlon in any other situation as far as I can tell."

"By the way," I wrote back, "was your grandmother, Katherine Leonard [Edward Ehrlich's second wife] a school teacher? Sarah Carver said that Edward Joseph ("Joe") Ehrlich II told her he decided he didn't want anything more to do with his father after he ran off with a school teacher. Alice Lloyd (alias Woods) certainly was a school teacher, and was studying to be a teacher when she hitched up with Edward J. Ehrlich I.

"None of the Joseph Ehrlich's kids have any listed numbers, ditto for Fern Bates. What I did is pay for some intelius searches on line and then wrote about 20 letters to all the possible addresses I could find. I think Sarah Carver must have gotten a forwarded letter because the address and number she gave me in Spokane was not on my original list. I know some of the others got letters but I don't know to what address.

"You could probably call Sarah Carver. She asked me if it was OK to tell 'Joe and Laura' about me."

"No, Katherine was in secretarial work," Denise wrote back. "Supposedly, she also played the piano for silent movie performances. You would not believe the collection of sheet music I have from 1885 through the 1940's. All of the Leonard children played the piano and other instruments. When did Alice Lloyd marry Lloyd Flood? It would seem Joe Ehrlich was too young to declare he did not want anything to do with Edward Ehrlich at the time he and Alice were involved with one another.

"I will have to make time to call Sarah — also Tom Conlon, and Connie.

"Denise Ehrlich"

"Bingo!" I wrote. "The school teacher was Alice Lloyd. The Schemmels probably told Joe Ehrlich that he dumped them at their house because he took off with a school teacher, and that was his justification in his mind for why he wasn't with his father. My mother was born in 1932 and the adoption papers say Alice was 'abandoned' by Edward J. Ehrlich I. Alice remarried in 1934 Lloyd Flood (more name dynamics!) which is when Alice Flood was born."

A week later I called Elinor back.

"I am having trouble dealing with this," she said. "A few weeks ago I didn't even know that I had a sister. Now I have to deal with the fact that she is dead."

After I hung up the phone I felt a shadow of sadness fall over me. Up to that time I had been buoyed along by the excitement of the genealogy chase. It was one thing to feel the loss of my own mother. That had always been a solo activity. But there was someone else that truly felt her loss. I felt sad, depressed and confused. What can of worms had I opened up?

To cheer myself up I logged on to ancestry.com and started to look for Alice's father in the census records of Wales.

Chapter 13

On September 27, 2006, "Curious" wrote the following letter to advice columnist Cary Tennis on salon.com:

"Dear Cary,

"My parents are obsessed with dead people.

"No, not ghosts. Genealogy.

"They are baby boomers and have been tracing their lineage for several years now. They are obsessed with their new hobby. This is strange because they are not the type to have obsessive interests. Every time I see them, they tell me about Great Great Uncle Jonas who died of smallpox or Great Great Grandma Enid who campaigned for the mayoral candidate of New York. At our last get-together, my mom talked so much I wondered if she was manic (although she has never had a mood disorder). I have never, at any point in my life, seen her this enthusiastic, even about anything that had to do with her children. This sounds like an exaggeration. Trust me, it's not.

"I find it sad that they appear to have no desire to cultivate their relationships on this earth (including with me), and instead spend their time tracking down people, regardless of what they have accomplished, they will never meet in the flesh. It's not that they don't socialize, it's just that they don't enjoy it and have no desire to become closer to the people around them. They used to be more tolerant, but now they don't like anyone and make no attempt to pretend otherwise.

"Why would healthy adults who are barely in their 60s become so attached to the past? They have the wealth that would allow them to travel and indulge in any other type of interest they desire right in the present. I'm sure plenty of seniors out there have expectations and dreams for the future, but not my folks. Is this something I'll understand when I'm their age? Or is this somehow a sign of sickness?

"Genealogy is a fascinating hobby, but I have limits. Any polite attempts I make to turn our conversation back to the present day so I can participate are rebuffed.

"It isn't my business how they live their lives, but it's thrown me for a loop seeing that they actually do have the capacity to care deeply about something. Why did it take this long?

"Curious"

Cary Tennis responded:

"Dear Curious,

"This sounds like a classic case of relative narcissism, a projection disorder in which the ego, unable to countenance its own narcissism, projects onto ancestors all the idealized qualities it would otherwise take onto itself; it is harder to diagnose than traditional narcissism because its sufferers do not act grandiose and superior. Rather, they adopt a humble air in deference to their great aunt or uncle. It's not they who are draped in glory but long-dead forebears (who, through genetic association, nevertheless give proof of superiority). It can be paired with a deep, melancholy longing for an idealized world and a sense that today's world can never measure up to this mythical past. It is often found in baby boomers who didn't attend Woodstock but had a cousin who did.

"Of course, you don't find "relative narcissism" in any diagnostic manual.

"It doesn't exist in the literature yet. I made it up.

"But if it did exist, it would exist because the psychiatric community would recognize that when an interest in one's ancestors becomes more than historical, when it seems to take over one's emotional life, then some need other than mere curiosity is being met. What is that need? What are they really getting out of it?...To contemplate the long line of people who preceded you might give you a sense of how vast time is, which is something like contemplating the ocean or the forest, something larger than oneself...

"The key question is: What are they getting out of it?

What indeed?

Chapter 14

I distracted myself from the existential angst of finding my living biological relatives by retreating to research of the dead ancestors of my father, a known quantity that wouldn't kick up any dust. My focus shifted to the Rockeys after I got an email from someone interested in that line of my family.

Madeline Ella Rockey, my grandmother's mother and the daughter of Thomas Jefferson Rockey, the Civil War veteran, was the original genealogy addict in our family, and the source of most of my genealogical information when I first started out.

Tim Sayers wrote to me about her family:

"I saw some information you posted on Ancestry that seems related to research that I am doing. Here's what I found:

"Name: Margaret Dautin

"Birth Date: 1773

"Birth Place: Maryland

"Death Date: 1876

"Death Place: Ill

"Do you have more information about this person that you could share with me?

"Thank you,

"I too descend from her and Barnet through their son Jacob Thomas Rockey." He gave me his email.

"Hi Tim," I responded.

"Margaret Dautin, b 16 Aug 1773 in Maryland, m 25 Mar 1807 Georges Valley (PA I think), d 10 Aug 1876 Rock Grove, Stephenson Co, Ill; Jacob Rockey b 02 Aug 1810 Pen Creek, Centre Co, Penn. I am descended from Abram Rockey b 22 Mar 1808 in Pen Creek, Centre Co, PA. The Rockeys moved eventually to Wash state where I was born. The gym at the high school in Olympia WA where I grew up was named for one of them, but now they are extinct by the male line in WA.

"No one really knows where they came from, although I think there was some talk about French Protestants.

"Most of the people in my family were Methodists, and they didn't seem to like to marry people from other religions, so I think they probably were, too.

"They were early pioneers in Centre Co PA and if you go to Tylersville; their graves are in a cemetery right by the highway. They are also mentioned in history of Centre Co. You can go to my website www.bremnerhistory.com to read what I have about them - the info I have on the tree is there as well."

"Doug," he replied.

"Are you aware that Margaret was half Delaware Indian? She was also one of 13 girls who stood in an archway as George Washington entered some town in Pennsylvania. I think the girls represented the 13 colonies. They were singing as he entered. I will be looking at your website.

"Tim."

I responded,

"I hadn't heard that. I had a genetic analysis done, and didn't turn up any Indian, although there was 4% African, which was a surprise. Below is the relevant text from the history of our family I wrote, mostly based on family stories passed down through my grandfather. It is on my site.

"Madeline Ella Rockey was born Sept. 6, 1873, in Lock Haven, Clinton Co., Pa. The Rockey family had a long history in Pennsylvania. The first recorded member of the family was David Rockey. The family was thought to be of French Huguenot origin (an earlier possible spelling variant "Raquet"). Another source lists David Rockey as a native of Ireland who came to this county and settled in Delaware County, Penn. (year not listed) and spent the last days of his life near Pleasant Gap, Centre Co., Penn. (Commemorative Biographical Record of Central Pennsylvania).

"There was a family tradition that an ancestor (father of Barnett Rockey) lived in Lancaster County, was Pennsylvania Dutch (or spoke the German current there) and fought in the American Revolutionary War, although his name is not known (either John, Peter or Michael Rockey (or Raquet)). The source for this information is a letter written in 1920 from a cousin John Rockey of Lebanon, Penn. to his cousin Madeline Rockey Bay [my great grandmother], then residing in Lynden, Washington. The son of this revolutionary soldier, Barnett Rockey (1772-1847) was born in Delaware County, Penn., raised in York County, Penn., and moved to Clinton County, Penn in about 1800. Per Hannah Howe, sister of Thomas Rockey, he was an orphan and had one known brother. He was remembered as speaking largely Pennsylvanian German since he was raised in the "Lancaster" area.

"Barnett Rockey married Margaret Dautin on March 25, 1807. Margaret Dautin Rockey was born in Maryland August 16, 1774, in a county near the Pennsylvania line. The source for that information is Lawrence Rockey of Freeport Illinois in a letter sent to Marian Bay Bremner [my grandmother]. Based on accounts from Hannah Howe, sister of Thomas Rockey, she was an orphan descended from a group of English who settled with Lord Baltimore in Maryland, who was raised by a Southern family who were slave owners. She had a sister and a brother who "went into the Virginia wilderness and were never heard from again.

"Barnett Rockey and Margaret Dautin Rockey had nine children between 1808 and 1826: Abraham, Jacob, Elizabeth, Michael, John, Susanne, Henry, David and William. Barnett Rockey learned the tanner's trade, and moved with his family to George's Valley near Spring Hill and Millheim, and worked as a laborer until 1818. They then moved to Brush Valley, near Spring Bank, and in 1826 to Sugar Valley, working as a farmer in both places. He died January 26, 1847, in Tylersville, Clinton County, Penn., and was buried in the cemetery in that town.

"Margaret Dautin Rockey moved with her children to Illinois, when she moved isn't clear. A newspaper clipping at the time of her death read, "Margaret Dautin Rockey was a native of

Maryland. She came to Illinois with her children in pioneer days, and passed away in 1876 at the age of 103 years. One incident of her life pointed to with pride is the fact that she participated in the inauguration of the first president, George Washington, being one of the group of ladies representing the states."

"Margaret died at the age of 102 in August 10, 1876, and is buried in the cemetery near Rock Grove, in Stephanson County, Illinois. One of their sons, Abraham Rockey, was born in Loganton, Clinton County, Penn., on March 22, 1808. He married Lydia Wommeldorf of Germantown PA on 5/11/1830 at Loganton PA. Lydia Wommeldorf was born to Frederick and Barbra Bierley Wommeldorf on Dec. 28, 1811.

"Little is known of the Wommeldorfs (Frederick was an orphan), the Biereleys came from Bavaria. Abraham Rockey and Lydia Wommeldorf Rockey had their first son, Paul, in Freeport, Ill., in 1831, and 12 more children up until 1857: Jacob, Rebecca, Jeremiah, John, Thomas Jefferson, Abraham Dautin, Lewis, William Barnett, Mary, James Bigler, Harriet J., Hannah Barbra. Several of the boys fought for the North in the Civil War.

"Abraham Rockey was mentioned in the History of Stephanson County: "Abraham Rockey was a farmer and proprietor of a sawmill, and made his home near Loganton, Clinton Co., Pa. He was called to his final rest on Feb. 10, 1865, when nearly 57 years of age. Both he and his wife belonged to the Evangelical Association." After the death of her husband, Lydia Wommeldorf remarried Frederick Seaver of

Sugar Valley, and died in Wisconsin, Sept. 2, 1892.

"Thomas Jefferson Rockey.

"One of the sons of Abraham Rockey and Lydia Wommeldorf Rockey was Thomas Jefferson Rockey, who was born in Loganton (Pleasantville), Clinton County, Pennsylvania, May 23, 1841. He fought for the North in the Civil War, was a sergeant of the First Pennsylvania Volunteer Cavalry Reserves, Company D, and was in a number of campaigns including the battles of Cedar Mountain, Gettysburg, Antietam, Bull Run, Chancellorsville, Brandywine Station, and Culpepper Courthouse. He took part in the famous cavalry charge of the Stonewall Brigade."

Tim replied, "Was the 4% African in the Rockey line?"

I replied, "There is no way to know that for sure, it can come from any ancestor. You can get yourself tested if you are interested, www.ancestrybydna.com."

Looking for information on the Rockeys, I found online a genealogy of the Descendants of Anthony Bierly and Lydia Womeldorf. I emailed the author for a copy and got the following response:

"Doug,

"Here is the information about my book. I am attaching my husband's direct line.

I will check the lineage you send and see what I can add.

"Thanks.

"Suzanne Rice"

I wrote back,

"I wrote a genealogy book as well and posted it at www.bremnerhistory.com

I will go through my tree and provide sources, specifically what came from my grandfather's genealogy of 1970, and what did not (i.e. unsourced information from rootsweb.com).

"Doug"

Suzanne Rice responded

"Thanks for the update. I have added some of the Thomas Jefferson ROCKEY family. I don't think I will do another book. The best to do now would be to put it on CD.

"When I started working on this, I didn't have enough computer space, so limited myself to families who stayed in PA. Now I have been adding all I find, and am up to 80,000 people. Of course, it is for all my husband's lines, not just BIERLY.

"I haven't gotten further back than Melchoir BIERLY, but do have the parents of Maria Anna Barbara OCKER, and the grandparents. I think that was on the list I sent you. I didn't do that research, so can't vouch for it.

"I do have more information on the WARNER/WERNER line.

"I am attaching an .rtf file. I have left my notes in.

"I haven't done a lot of work on this line. It is out of the area where I have the most research material.

"Doug BIERLY did the German research for the BIERLY line. He used to have a web page, but I can't find it. He sent me copies of German records, but I don't think determined the father of Melchoir.

"Suzanne"

80,000 names? Suzanne was obviously another genealogy addict.

A few days later I got the results of my mitochondrial DNA analysis in the mail, the one that would tell me who my ancestor was in the maternal line. Apparently, my original "Eve" probably came from Norway or somewhere in that general area. That fit with my research showing that my mother's grandmother on the maternal side was from Norway. It also meant that I was not "officially Jewish", at least if you went along with the view of most modern scholars on the topic.

I felt an urge to meet my lost relatives from Spokane. I emailed Denise Ehrlich and told her that I wanted to visit them over Christmas. She responded that she wanted to go as well, but had to work during that time period.

I contacted my parents. How about if we came to visit during Christmas of 2006? We could go to Bend, Oregon, near the ski resort of Mt Bachelor, and where my sister Anne had a condominium and where we had spent many Christmas vacations over the years. We could cut out for a couple of days to got Spokane and see the new relatives. I did a search on MapQuest and figured we could make it in five hours. Maybe we could leave the kids with their grandparents.

I was worried that going to visit my mother's biological family in Spokane would upset my parents. I hoped that if we left our kids with them and were gone for as short a time as possible that there wouldn't be any problems.

It was with a mixture of excitement and dread that I went about making plans for a trip to Spokane, Washington.

Chapter 15

Later that month, I attended a party at the Georgia Aquarium in Atlanta, GA. It was held in conjunction with a scientific meeting I was attending at the convention center in town that week, and was hosted by the psychiatry department at Emory University School of Medicine, where I am a professor. The Georgia Aquarium, only a few years old, is the largest Aquarium in the world.

We stood around chatting and drinking cocktails. Immense Right whales swam past behind a massive wall of glass, followed by schools of fish of all different colors and sizes. I saw a colleague whom I knew was Jewish, and approached her to bring up my favorite topic of conversation.

"I had a genetic analysis done and did some genealogical research, and found out that I am one third Jewish," I said.

She looked a little taken aback. I guess she didn't peg me as the Jewish type, or maybe she didn't want me as part of her ethnic group.

"Was your mother Jewish?"

"Since she was adopted I don't know for sure," I replied. "But I think her grandmother was Norwegian."

"Then you aren't really Jewish."

"But a Rabbi said 'being a learned and scholarly man is a better sign of who is a Jew than who your mother is.'" I was becoming a regular expert on Judaism, after reading *Finding Your Jewish Parents* and trolling on the internet.

"But that's not how the rules go," she said.

"Actually, those rules are based on the time of the return from exile in Babylon to Jerusalem. Everyone was confused about who was who, so they set up these series of rules that determined how 'Jewish' you were. Men with non-Jewish wives were still considered Jews, just less so than those with Jewish wives. Besides, modern genetic studies show that the original 'Eve' of most Jewish families was an ethnic native of the country the moved to." In other words Jewish men left Israel, mated with native women, and then started a unique Jewish population group in that country.

She looked at me in a funny way. I went back to the food table and got another appetizer.

We made the trip out to Bend, Oregon, in December of 2006. After a couple of days of skiing, my wife and I left our kids with my parents, and drove to Spokane to see my 'other' family. Given the awkwardness of the situation, I arranged only two days for the trip, so we would drive up one day and return the next.

Elinor Iverson had arranged for us to stay at the Davenport Hotel in Spokane. This was a classic old hotel that had recently been renovated. Ironically, it was also the hotel where Edward Ehrlich worked as a young man as a busboy, and where his mother, Catherine "Emma" Powers, was a waitress. Alice Lloyd's father also worked there, so it was likely that was where Alice and Edward met. It felt ironic that Elinor was setting my wife and I up for a 'honeymoon suite' at her expense at the very hotel that was the source of my existence in the first place.

As we drove North, I took pleasure in watching the wheat fields (now all stubs in the month of December, partially covered with snow) roll past outside our car windows. My wife and I had traveled in Eastern Washington before, tooling around the coulees, vast canyons carved out by the breaking of an ancient dam that broke in middle Montana at the end of the last ice age 10,000 years ago and flooded out all of the rivers of Eastern Washington State. On other trips, we had cruised through vast flat plains of the Great Basin of Eastern Washington, Eastern Oregon and Nevada, broken only by the sage brush, travelled the hills and deserts of the High Desert region around Bend, Oregon, or followed the rushing rivers of the enigmatic John Day country in the Northern part of Eastern Oregon up by the Columbia River Valley.

The closer we came to Spokane, the faster my heart beat. I had never been to Spokane, a medium sized city that abutted the border with Oregon. I knew it was the hub where the products of the harvest of the vast plains of wheat were transported, the "Inland Empire", and had always imagined that it would have a similar terrain as the rest of Eastern Washington.

That is why I was surprised to see the country change, becoming more mountainous, with pine trees. I now realized it was located in the foothills of the Rocky Mountains. As I was later to learn, there are in fact some very good ski areas within a half hour of Spokane that are located in the Rocky Mountains.

A sign on the freeway said, "Four Lakes".

"My mother and her family lived there when she was a baby," I told my wife. "Let's stop there for a minute."

We pulled off the freeway. The town consisted of a series of trailers and dowdy prefabricated homes. Apart from a tavern there was no evidence of a business district. The Four Lakes Elementary School, where the Coopers once taught, was long gone.

"They should call this town Four Trailers instead of Four Lakes," I told my wife. She laughed.

We turned back onto the freeway and headed toward Spokane.

We followed the directions toward the Davenport Hotel. As we pulled into the hotel, it felt a little weird. This was obviously the premier hotel in town. I was used to staying in high-end hotels in New York or Washington DC— but in Spokane, Washington? The fact that it could have been the site of my grandparents' illicit mating scene also made the situation even more weird.

After we checked in, we called Elinore. She gave us directions to her house. We drove out through the city and into the suburbs. After a few wrong turns we ended up outside her house. She made motions for where we should park in her driveway like an employee of an airport waving in a 747.

We walked in to her house and sat on the sofa, facing off against her, her son and daughter-in-law. An artificial Christmas tree blinked at as from the other side of the room.

"Would you like something to drink? She said.

"I'm fine."

I cast a side long glance at my Italian born wife. This was probably the last place she imagined she would end up at this point in her life. She managed a wan smile.

"You have a very nice place here," my wife said.

"Garage door wouldn't open with the last freeze," said her son, Barry (my... cousin? I couldn't keep it all straight at this point}

"So what can you tell us about your mother?" my wife said (her mother also being my grandmother).

"Well, I don't know," said Elinore.

"Are we going to do the trip for the classic car show this year?" said her son.

"I think we better go to be on time for our dinner reservations," said Elinore. "We have reservations at a very nice restaurant with views of the Spokane Falls."

After we got to the restaurant, we huddled around the menus. A round of drinks made things seem to go a little smoother. After dinner the waitress took a group photo. We all said good bye and made promises to stay in touch.

Chapter 16

The next day my wife and I left the Davenport Hotel for our pre-arranged meeting with the other side of the family, the Ehrlichs. We had been given specific instructions for how to drive to the house of Connie Martin (wife of Lannie Martin, daughter of Tom Conlon, and granddaughter of Harold (Hal) Conlon, who had been born Hal Ehrlich, brother to Edward Joseph Ehrlich I and son of Jacob Ehrlich and Emma Powers. Connie had told me that Jacob abandoned the family when Hal was a child, and he never saw him again, apart from a brief encounter when he was in college.

From my discussions on the phone with Connie, I had the feeling that she didn't care about the details of where I came from, if you were family you were welcome and you should come down and visit. She previously suggested that we come during the summer, so that Tom Jr., her brother the dentist, could take us all out on his boat on one of the many lakes around Spokane. That didn't fit in with my Italian wife's plans to make an annual pilgrimage to visit her family in Italy, so we had to delay the trip.

As we followed the directions for our pre-arranged meeting with the Martins we travelled away from the center of Spokane and up into the hills surrounding the city. Up in the hills, everything was covered with snow. As I maneuvered around the hairpin turns in the hills I became increasingly worried about my ability to make it up the steep hills in my rental car.

We finally arrived in front of the house of the Martins, their driveway completely sheeted with ice.

When they saw us pull up they came out of the front door.

"Why don't you come on in for a minute?" said Connie's husband, Lannie Martin, who was standing in the driveway, balancing a cup of coffee in one hand.

My wife and I parked the car and slid across the icy driveway toward the front door of their house. We gingerly opened the door and let ourselves in.

"Do you have time to sit down for a minute?" said Lannie.

"Sure, I think so," I said.

My wife and I sat next to each other on the couch.

We talked about our family connections. Connie pulled out a photo album that came from her father.

"This is a picture of Edward Joseph Ehrlich I when he was a young man," she said.

He was standing with a thin and very pretty young woman, with dark black hair.

"That must be Laura Schemmel!" I said

"Here is a picture of my father, Tom Conlon, when he was young," she said.

Who is that pretty young woman with him?" I asked.

"I don't know," she said, turning the page.

"There he is again, with a different young woman!"

She turned the page.

"And another one!"

"He was a star football player in college, and a handsome man as well. I guess he had a lot of girlfriends."

Lannie asked me what I was up to.

"Well I'm trying to trace the history of my family. And some of those people are here in Spokane."

"In your email you said you wanted to find their graves."

"Yes, that's right"

"Do you want to go now?"

"Yes I do." I was getting worried about the time.

We all piled into Lannie's SUV. I started to look in my palm pilot. I found out where some of the ancestors were buried.

"Joseph and Julia Ehrlich were buried at the Mt. Nebo Cemetery. Do you know where that is?" I asked. These were the grandparents of Edward Joseph Ehrlich I, our common ancestors who were the original immigrants to America.

"Yes I do," said Connie. "I have driven by there a hundred times. Although I knew that my grandparents were buried there, I never went in."

"Well now is your chance," I said.

I had a good feeling. I felt that these people were put here by destiny to help me find a piece of something I had been looking for my entire life. A missing piece of the puzzle from my past. The puzzle that was myself.

What would Joseph Smith say?

We pulled into the driveway of the cemetery. There was a large iron gate over the entrance with the Star of David. We all stared in shock.

"Do you have any doubts about your Jewish ancestry now?" I asked.

We pulled into the cemetery and parked. As we got out of the car, I had a surreal feeling. All of the headstones had Hebrew writing on them. If there had been any doubts about Jewish ancestry before, they were gone now.

I followed the stone number that I had looked up on the internet. Suddenly I found it.

"Here it is!" I called out.

A large stone spelled out the name EHRLICH in block letters. We scraped away the snow over two stone markers set into the ground.

FATHER

JOSEPH EHRLICH

NOV. 11, 1853

SEPT 3, 1931

Next to it was

MOTHER

JULIA EHRLICH

APR. 18, 1856

MAY 20, 1919

We all stood and contemplated the scene. My wife took a picture of me next to the head

stones.

We got in the car and drove to the Fairmount Memorial Park, where, ironically, both my grandmother, Alice Pauline Lloyd Flood, and Connie's father, Hal Conlon, were buried, even though they probably never knew each other.

Connie led us to the place where Hal Conlon and his wife, Eva, were buried. She knew the general location, but the ground was covered in snow and ice. We tried to scrape the snow and ice away, but we couldn't find the stone that was set in the ground.

We next looked for Alice. After poking around several memorial buildings, which held crypts with interred ashes, we finally found her. She was interred in a wall facing directly toward the lovely Spokane River Canyon.

In the stone was engraved

BELOVED WIFE & MOTHER

ALICE P. FLOOD

1912-1990

I stood by the stone to have my picture taken by my wife.

I quipped, "Beloved mother to some, but not all."

Next to Alice was her husband, Lloyd Flood.

I turned to look at the Spokane River Canyon. Alice certainly had found a nice resting spot with an excellent view. The roaring water a thousand feet below made a majestic scene. Pine trees littered the banks rising up from the river far below. It was cold but the sky was a brilliant blue and the air was sparkling.

I wondered if Alice ever could have imagined that her offspring would catch up with her here. Probably not. But then she probably never conceived of the fact that the new, divinely inspired creation of a technology called the internet would ever become as extensive as it was today.

I wonder if Joseph Smith ever saw it in one of his prophetic visions of the future?

Chapter 17

On the way back from Spokane, we drove through the town of Reardan, Spokane, where my mother, Elinore, and their biological mother, Alice, had acted out their drama sixty years before. A large grain silo with the words REARDAN GRAIN GROWERS INC. written across it dominated the town skyline.

Apart from that, there was only a gas station and a few abandoned store fronts. A clutch of flat roofed houses surrounded the silos. Beyond the town stretched a flat, treeless, snow-covered expanse of ground. We drove a little out of town and I got out of the car. The ground gently undulated away in all directions. I imagined a sea of wheat that would come in the summer.

"Hardly seems enough to have merited a school house, let alone all of that drama that those people went through," I said to my wife.

We got back in the car and headed south to Bend.

When we got back the mood at the condo with my parents was tense.

"Why did you feel the need to look for them," my step-mother said. "You've never gotten over the death of your mother. When are you going to move on?"

"I just want to learn more about where I came from," I said. "I think that is only natural. Everybody wants to know where they came from."

"But when are you going to move on? You've been dwelling on this for twenty years. When are you going to move on?"

She was really insistent.

"Okay, now," I said. "I am going to move on right now. As of right now I am over the death of my mother."

"I don't believe you," she said. "You're stuck on the death of you mother. You've never accepted me as your mother. You've always been stuck on the death of your mother."

"I have accepted you as my mother," I said. "Wasn't I the first person in our family to call you mom? The fact is that my mother died when I was four years old. I have only a vague memory of her. You were my mother for most of my life. You were there when I started school, when I played my first baseball game. You played that role. There is nothing that can take that away from you."

"But you never gave me a strong hug. You always have been so detached."

"That's the way he is," my wife said. "I don't rely on him to give me a strong hug to know that he loves me. He lets me know in other ways."

The next day we flew back to Atlanta.

Chapter 18

The day after we got home, I logged on to my computer. My doug@bremnerhistory.com email had a bunch of messages to respond to. I gave Denise Ehrlich an update on the trip to Spokane. I also had a message from someone named Jayne Overgard, who had found me through the web site for Jewish genealogy, JewGen.com. She wrote:

"Subject: Family Tree of the Jewish People: William HASKELL

"My mother-in-law is descended from John Haskell b. 1670 Middleboro, MA, married Mary Squire on 2 Mar 1698. Any Information you have would be appreciated.

"Thanks!

I replied,

"You should look at the book series, *Mayflower Increasings*, which has a book on George Soule and his descendants and *The Great Migration Begins*, which includes information on Soul and John Haskell, as I remember [both books include comprehensive information on the first few generations of people descended from the original passengers of the ships, *Mayflower* and *Anne*, that brought the first immigrants to New Plymouth in New England in 1620 and 1623]. Also the *History of Plymouth*, by Thatcher, and the book on Plymouth by William Bradford [leader of the Pilgrims, or the Separatists, as they called themselves at the time]."

Jayne responded,

"Thank you so much for the response, and the book recommendations.

"Can you tell me about the Haskells being Jewish? My mother-in-law had been told they were, but by the time she came along (maiden name also Haskell), they were some flavor of protestant Christian. We are interested in the migration and the history.

"Thanks in advance,

"Jayne Overgard"

I replied:

"That's pretty interesting. If you have any more documentation on that I would appreciate it. Family lore can be strikingly correct or very wrong. I am genetically one third Jewish, although I have only one great-grandfather who is known to be Jewish (I didn't find out about him until last year, previously I thought I was completely gentile until I got my DNA tested). Based on that, I should be one eighth Jewish (or less, by genetics, since most Jews trace their maternal line to a gentile original mother). His son became an apostate and denied ever being Jewish.

"I tracked down my great-great-grandfather in a Jewish cemetery in Spokane, Washington, last year. I think there are many people in the U.S. descended from apostate Jews. Many of my ancestors were Germans from Pennsylvania, and I suspect many were apostate Jews. George Soule, who is the ancestor of Haskell, came to Plymouth in 1623 on the *Ann* so he is one of the 'old comers' [the name given by the residents to people who descended from the original passengers on the *Ann* and the *Mayflower*]. You should buy *George Soule* in the *Mayflower Risings* book series, which is available in paperback from the New England Genealogical Society. It lists him and all of his descendants. Also in *The Great Migration Begins,* by Robert Charles Anderson, published by the New England Genealogical Society, it lists him and all recorded information about him. You can get these books at www.abebooks.com. I probably have repeated it on my website with my family genealogy www.bremnerhistory.com in the chapter on Clarks and Freeman

I attached a couple more family trees that have information about the siblings of the Haskells etc."

Jayne wrote:

"Doug,

"Thanks so much again for your response. I am attaching what I have on her family from John Haskell. Your information is very interesting as well. I just found out last week that I am about 1/16 Jewish but may be closer to 1/8 or 1/4. Imagine!! I am obviously just in the infancy of discovery on this but I am so fascinated. All of mine would have converted to Lutheran in Germany. Mine are from the vicinity of Stuttgart, a few miles away, and here are some of the surnames: Noerdlinger, Ziegler, Walther and Walter, Silber, Lehmann, Salzer, Handel, Reusch, Veil or Veihel, Scherer, Schilling, Haas, Rath, maybe others. I wonder what it was like for them? I imagine that they traveled and to fit in and do business and survive and be trusted they had to join the church. But I am very new at this and would like to be corrected if incorrect....

"Thanks so much,

"Jayne"

I replied:

"Attached is a picture of me in a Jewish cemetery in Spokane, WA, of all places, where I tracked down the gravestone of my great-great-grandfather. My mother was adopted, and even though I had the adoption papers opened 15 years ago, the parents lied about their names on the certificate, which made it difficult to follow my family tree. However they told 'partial truths', so I was able to figure it out eventually with help from the local genealogy society. However, based on my genetics test, I think there is Jewish blood on my father's side, either through Pennsylvania 'Germans' or extra-marital activity in other parts of the family. I am going back and referencing things now (including using References to the family's historical genealogy) because I have found that many things on ancestry.com and other places are wrong, including information in the registries. If I get information from another person I simply reference that person.

"All of the Haskell stuff is pretty well documented in *The Great Migration Begins* as are all of the early arrivals in Plymouth, since they were obsessive record keepers. I just haven't gotten around to putting in all of the references for those people. It has been a pretty interesting experience tracking down all of these elusive Jews. As one of my new-found cousins said, those people must be flipping in their graves over having all of their secrets uncovered.

"When I first found out that my grandfather was named Ehrlich, I did an internet search, and was shocked to get a list of rabbis and scholars of the Talmud. My great-grandfather was Jacob Ehrlich, which turned out to be the real name of Perry Mason. When I called his grandson he was freaked out, because Jacob Ehrlich was a womanizer, and he was worried about new family members popping up. Turned out he was the wrong one. My great-grandfather was born in Bohemia, and was an acknowledged Jew, and then abandoned his family in Spokane. I have never been able to track him down.

"I have found that the Jews that went to the Northeast stayed in their community. However, many Jews who wanted to get away from the Shtetl life, where they were basically prisoners in their towns in Europe, took the opportunity of migration to abandon their Jewishness. They preferentially went to the West Coast, some through Canada.

"They found through genetic testing that about half the Hispanics who were the original Mexican settlers in New Mexico were apostate Jews. I think a similar phenomenon may have occurred with the migration of many Germans in the 19th century, although no one has looked at that, as far as I know.

"Here are a couple of books: *Finding Our Fathers A Guidebook to Jewish Genealogy*, by Dan Rottenberg. *The Great Migration Begins to New England, 1620-1633* by Robert Charles

Anderson. This has the complete information on the original Haskell."

"Doug,

"Thanks for the picture. It's all so fascinating!! Several of my ancestors started in Pennsylvania, so I'm opening up all of my research now. My mother's grandfather came over to America in 1860 to escape some "religious persecution," but I just assumed it was some sort of Lutheran/Catholic clash. I can't find him anywhere...

"Anyway, I thought I was three fourths German... looking into it all now. The rest of me is one fourth Norwegian (you probably could have guessed from my name...).

"Thanks for all the stories and suggestions. I'll be ordering some books this week!

"So, Doug, is it your understanding that John Haskell was Jewish? Or was he just in your family tree? Thanks, Jayne.

I replied,

"Was the information about your family being Jewish passed on by family tradition?"

"Yes, the information was researched in the days before the internet by Burt Hughes, a descendant. He got it from the New England Historical and Genealogical Register Volume LXXVI (volume number almost unreadable). It begins with William Haskell, a church warden in 1627 in Charlton-Musgrave, Somerset, England buried there 12, May 1630.

"Jayne"

I got a package in the mail from Diane Sams. It was the research I had asked her to do two years ago. She had appropriately identified Edward Joseph Ehrlich as my grandfather. She also included a copy of the legal paperwork for the divorce proceedings of Jacob Ehrlich and Emma Powers Ehrlich. It described how Tom Conlon was living in a boarding house owned by Jacob Ehrlich and Emma Powers Ehrlich. How Jacob and Tom got into a fight and Jacob moved out. Emma later married Tom Conlon. Was Tom a marriage breaker? I don't think anyone knew that part of the history.

Diane also provided an obituary for Mable Pauline Woods. Born in 1912 in Okanogan, Washington, she would have been the right age to be my mother's mother. Diane claimed that she was in the Spokane Directory and was listed as working at the Dessert Hotel as a waitress, the same hotel where Edward Joseph Ehrlich had worked. However she didn't include a copy of the city directory.

She also provided an obituary, which listed Nancy Hall of Renton, Washington, as a surviving daughter.

Was this the real Alice?

I gave Diane a call.

"Why the different name?" I asked.

"A lot of times people made up a new name if there was someone working in the same place who had the same name. It was a pretty common practice at that time. Edith Gilbert may only have known her by that name, and it was Edith who filled out the paperwork for the adoption."

"But I have this other Alice I have identified. Which do you think is the correct one?"

"You never can know for sure, but I think Mable is probably the correct one."

I hung up the phone. My genealogy obsession was back. I had to know for sure.

I did a USSearch for a Nancy Hall of Renton, Washington. I found a couple of candidates and called up my best one.

"I am doing research on my family tree and want to see if we might be related," I said, repeating my old drill.

"OK," she said. "Go ahead."

"Are you related to Mable Pauline Woods?" I asked.

"Yes, she was my mother,"

"Did she ever go by the name Alice?"

"Not that I know of."

"Or live in Spokane?"

"Not that I know of."

"What happened to your father, Frank Woods?"

"I was born in Okanogan, Washington. When I was a child my father drank a lot. He was fine when he was sober, but that wasn't very often. He and my mother divorced shortly after I was born and she remarried."

"OK, so I guess she probably is not the right one. But do you mind if I call you again?"

"Sure, no problem."

172

After I hung up the phone I thought about it. Vinnie Cooper, my mother's half sister, had identified Elinor Flood as my mother's half-sister. My wife said I looked like her. Why was I off tracking new Alices? Was there something about the quest itself that I yearned for?

It seemed like many of my genealogy crazed cyberspace contacts were members of the Mormon Church (aka the Latter Day Saints, or LDS). I wanted to know more. What drove these people? How did their faith drive their interest in genealogy? Why was genealogy part of their religion? Could the answers to these questions answer my questions about myself, and what drove me?

Jayne Overgard, my Haskell contact, had citations to the ancestral file system that was used by the Mormons to keep track of who had been baptized posthumously in the church. I assumed she was a member of the church, so I thought I would start with her.

I wrote to Jayne,

"I noticed you had some LDS references. Are you part of the LDS church? I am asking because, although I am not part of the LDS church, I am interested in learning about how they organize their genealogy program."

"Doug,"

"First, yes, I see the Hebrew in the picture and the Stars of David (she was referring to me in the Jewish cemetery in Spokane next to the tomb stone of Joseph Ehrlich, my great-great-grandfather).

"Secondly, no, I'm not part of the LDS church. I used the familysearch site for some information.

"Jayne"

I was stunned. How could someone who seemingly spent her life steeped in the esoterica of genealogy, who thoroughly knew the LDS web sites, who obviously spent hours on line in genealogy research, not be a member of the LDS church, for whom genealogy research was a sacred duty?

Was there a segment of the population who was not LDS affiliated, but who was nevertheless obsessed with genealogy research? If so, what did it mean for them? Was it religious then, or what?

I sat and pondered this question. What did genealogy mean for people? I mean, emotionally, if it was not part of an established religion? And if it did have an emotional or quasi-religious meaning for people outside of an established religion, what was this all about? Why had I become so obsessed with the topic, and why were there so many people like me out there?

I decided to call my original Muse. Charles Hansen, Director of Research for the Eastern Washington Genealogical Society (EWGS). He had been my first contact for finding out critical information about my family roots in Spokane. He was quoted as an important source of information by a book that came from the LDS church.

If he didn't have an answer to the question *what does genealogy mean? ... and why do people do it?* then who would?

This kind man had tirelessly looked up Spokane obituaries for me on the Ehrlich clan. I saw him quoted in a book called *Genealogy Resources*, which listed where to go for genealogy information on a state-by-state basis. I originally found his name while trolling rootsweb.com for information on how to research Spokane ancestors. It was there that I found a post mentioning a kind man in Spokane who would look things up for you.

Charles is an accountant in Spokane, Washington. He volunteers as a researcher for the Eastern Washington Genealogical Society (EWGS). That means that people look him up on rootsweb.com or other internet sites and email him to ask him to go look up their ancestor's obituary in the Spokane newspaper (called the Spokesman Review) in the library, or go look up a birth or death certificate in the Spokane County Courthouse.

Charles spends many hours each weak looking up information for people he doesn't know. Charles told me that the LDS sponsored book *Genealogy Resources* contacted him thinking that he was the President of the EWGS, but he told them "he would rather be a genealogical researcher than the president."

In addition to Charles, the EWGS staffs a group of "genies" (a nickname derived from the word genealogy) who hang out in the Spokane Public Library at set times every week. They help novice researchers find the resources they need in the library to research their family trees. Charles and his group are also volunteers in the quest to transcribe all of the Washington State birth, marriage and death certificates, as well as census data, so that it can be posted on the internet.

Is this pure sacrifice? Or is there a higher power that drives him to do this? I know nothing in the Bible that says thou shalt look up the obituaries of strangers that send you emails with such requests. At least not in the original Bible. So what drives him to this altruistic behavior?

Brimming with anticipation, I looked up Charles in the Spokane phone book (or more accurately whitepages.com) and gave him a call.

My main question was... what does genealogy _mean_ to Charles Hansen? I asked him if I could interview him for a possible book on genealogy, and he agreed.

"You are a volunteer for the EWGS," I said. "You spend several hours or more each week looking things up for people for no pay. What motivates you to do it? What got you interested in genealogy?" I asked.

"I can't really say," he responded in a reserved way.

Surely this was not going to be the man who would enlighten me about this phenomenon that seemed to be gripping segments of the American population. I felt at a loss.

"How about your own family?" I countered. "Have you done research on them? How did you get interested in doing research on your own family genealogy?"

"Well, in 1991 we had a family reunion of the Hansen family in Spokane, Washington."

I felt that Charles was starting to warm up about the source of his passion for genealogy.

"Before the reunion I compiled a list of relatives and their addresses. I wrote to them and gave them blank family group sheets (a blank form that you can fill out family trees) and asked them to fill out as much information as possible, including children names, birth and marriage dates, and so on. I also asked them to send copies to relatives of theirs that I didn't know about. I got 350 family sheets returned. I was amazed."

"So how many people were you able to add to your family," I asked.

"It was about 1800."

"And do you use a particular software to enter your family tree data on a computer?"

"I use path software, and ancestralquest."

"When did you start doing active research?"

"At the reunion in 1991 I met one of my second cousins, her name was Loraine Erikson. She was a member of the LDS church. She had a family group sheet to fill in the names of her ancestors, but there were a lot of missing spaces. We thought we could try and do some research to fill in the missing spaces.

"So I went back into my family history. I found that my Great Grandfather was born in Denmark. His name was Hans Mikkelsen. His children's last names were Hansen, which meant "son of Hans". At that time in Denmark last names were "son of [father's name]."

"I went to Denmark and did some research on Hans Mikkelsen. He was from the village of Humble, on the island of Laangland. It is a long thin island near the coast of Germany. He lived in a Hus according to the civil records, which is defined as a small farm of less than five acres. He was listed as making clothing and shoes, and with five children it must have been difficult to eke out a living. I also found out that Denmark was on the brink of war with Germany at that time, and for that reason there was a universal draft for 18 year old males in Denmark at that time. The war with Germany did not happen, but that probably influenced the fact that four of the sons of Hans Mikkelsen emigrated to America on their 17th birthdays.

"Using civil records I was able to trace the lineage of Hans back four generations. They would list the names of the parents and the date of birth of the child, so it was easy to trace the records back. After four generations, however, the civil records stopped, and I had to go church records. A couple of generations back the hand of the priest writing in the records became so shaky that I couldn't trace it back anymore.

"The sons of Hans included Peter, Anton (my grandfather), John, Lawrence, and Martin. They all emigrated to American. Two other daughters and two brothers died young in Denmark, so there was no surviving family in Denmark. All of the emigrating brothers except my grandfather stayed in Minnesota. My grandfather had the urge to move around a lot. He didn't like living on the farm in Minnesota so he moved on to Montana when my father was three. When my father grew up he didn't like living on the farm, so he moved to Northern Idaho where he worked for a timber company, first as a cook's helper, and later hauling logs, first with horses, and later with a Model T, a Model A, and later a Ford V8. Later we moved to

Spokane, Washington, where I was born, and where he worked selling cars. I have lived in Spokane my entire life."

"What has been the most interesting thing you have found through your research?" I asked.

"Well, I was surprised I had so many relatives in Minnesota," he said. "My grandfather never said much about his family. He always said you should speak English, not Danish. But four out of the five of the original immigrant brothers stayed in Minnesota, and we never knew about them, or about all of their descendants. I was amazed when I found all of these people through my research."

"Why do you think people are going mad about genealogy now?" I asked.

"When people get a certain age, they become interested in family and where they went. I guess it is the baby boomers growing up. They are getting to the age where they wonder where they came from, and who their extended family is."

After I hung up the phone with Charles, I got a feeling for where the passion for his interest in genealogy was coming from. These were real people, who had rough necked their way around the American West, and were gone now, except through the thin transcripts of birth records and vital statistics. By researching these people, Charles was making them come alive. And their lives were really lively.

I thought about my own obsession. Why had I kept on so relentlessly for over a year looking for my roots? Why did I have a hard time giving up the Rosenbergs and the Hurns, even after I learned that they weren't part of my family? Why did I feel happy thinking about Sarah Eleanor Lee Wilson lying in her place of repose in a weed entangled graveyard by the side of a lonely Indiana highway? Why was I glad that Alice Pauline Lloyd Flood had such a pleasant view of the Spokane River Gorge? Why did I take up with the search for Mable Pauline Woods, when the evidence was against her being a possible ancestor? Why were all these people spending so much time to photograph tombstones, plow through musty records, type names into software programs, spend their vacations on family quests?

I thought about Charles again. He lit up when he told the story of his own family. I connected with him when I listened to the story of the Danish brothers who emigrated to the American West. I connected with Jeanie McEldowney when she told the story of the Aunt who took care of her disabled veteran husband Fred Gran. I separated their names from my Family Tree Maker file called "Bremner", but kept them as a separate file called "Woods."

Then I realized it was all about stories. Stories about people who came from another country, who had children, worked toward their dreams, had real set backs and real disappointments, as well as real triumphs. It was stories about people who lived real lives. Genealogy was about not letting those lives go, not letting those lives be lived in vain, about honoring their existence, and not letting their spirits slip away into the mist.

And it didn't necessarily have anything to do with religion.

Or did it?

I emailed Charles,

"Thanks for your help, Charles. By the way, could you look up some names in the Spokane City Directory for me?"

Postscript

Believe it or not, this story didn't end here. You can read about what happened next in this book:

The Goose That Laid the Golden Egg: Accutane – the truth that had to be told

You can find links to purchase the "Goose" book and all of my books in ebook or paperback form at:

www.dougbremner.com/laughingcowbooks.html

To see pictures of my mother and the rest of my family, you can go to this web site:

www.bremnerhistory.com/laurnellbremner.html

Here's a picture of me and my kids about twenty years ago at Coon Lake, Washington, near Stehekin.

Feel free to contact me with corrections or to give feedback about what you thought about the book and your own obsessions, genealogical or otherwise. My contact information is on my website www.dougbremner.com where you will find links to my blog and other pages.

Be sure to visit my facebook page "Doug Bremner" (writer) and "like" it, and check back for upcoming books on an ever diverging tangent of topics.

You can also follow our independent feature comedy film "Catania!" that I wrote and directed by looking for its facebook page by searching for "Catania the movie".

My blog is at www.beforeyoutakethatpill.com, the feed is www.beforeyoutakethatpill.com/index.php/feed, and I am on twitter as @dougbremner.